How to Make Books with Children

SCIENCE & MATH

Author: Joy Evans
Editor: Bob DeWeese and
   Jo Ellen Moore
Cover Design: Cheryl Kashata
Illustrator: Joy Evans
Production Asst: Michelle Tapola

Entire contents copyright ©1995 by EVAN-MOOR CORP.
18 Lower Ragsdale Drive, Monterey, CA 93940-5746

Evan-Moor
EDUCATIONAL PUBLISHERS

Table of Contents

Introduction

Student-Authored Science Books

Student-Authored Math Books

Writing Forms and Patterns

Binding Tips

Ring Binding

Metal rings inserted through a hole-punched sheet are a quick and easy way to bind papers into a book form. This method allows for easy reorganization of materials. It also will hold a large number of stories and opens flat on a table.

Tied Binding

A binding may be tied with ribbon, string or cord. This method of binding may also be undone to allow for changes. A cloth cover, a construction paper cover or a tagboard or cardboard cover may be used. If a heavy material is used that doesn't bend or fold easily, it is wise to provide a hinged front cover to allow for frequent opening and closing. (See below.)

The tying may be done in several ways:
• multiple ties
• wrapped tying

Sewn Binding

Either hand or machine sewing can be used to create a secure binding. The number of pages should be limited to allow the needle to access all layers.

This sort of binding also requires a cover that is either hinged to allow easy opening or use of a flexible paper or fabric.

Stapled or Paper-Fastened Binding

These two methods are the most common sort of classroom binding techniques. Student or classroom books can be constructed quickly by stapling or securing with paper fasteners. A hinged cover would lend flexibility to this technique. Either of these techniques can be improved by the addition of cloth tape to cover the bound spine of the book.

Hinged Binding

This type of binding is very useful in providing a cover that looks impressive and offers sturdy but easy access to the stories.

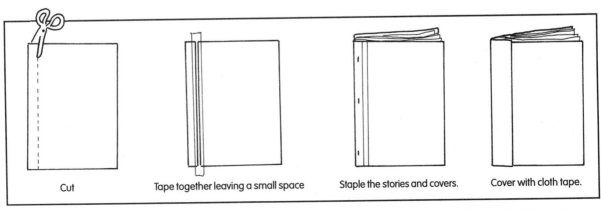

| Cut | Tape together leaving a small space | Staple the stories and covers. | Cover with cloth tape. |

The Writing Process

Brainstorm   Write   Edit

Students learn to write by writing. The classroom situation provides a stimulus and a time to learn the basic skills that make writing successful. Math and science are areas of the curriculum that can be rich resources for topics that motivate writing.

Brainstorm

Always introduce a writing topic with a brainstorming period. Get students committed to the subject by enlisting their opinions and questions they want answered. Find out what they already know and where they can find further information.

Brainstorming is also the time where new vocabulary is introduced. Make lists of words that apply to a topic. Encourage students to keep their own list of vocabulary they encounter that is new or interesting.

Rough Draft

When beginning to write, it is important that the ideas be allowed to flow freely. The writer should not dwell on spelling or punctuation. The concept should be developed so that the ideas are clear. This step in the writing process sets the purpose of the written piece.

Edit

The editor's job is to read the rough draft and determine where the author needs to make corrections. The editor may be the teacher or it may be a fellow student. Now is the time to make changes in spelling and punctuation and to clarify incomplete ideas.

Final Draft

The final draft of a written piece should show concern for correctness in spelling, punctuation and penmanship. This draft will have illustrations added and has as its ultimate goal the idea of sharing it with other readers.

Student-Authored

SCIENCE BOOKS

Where Did It Come From?

A Book in a Box

Project:

Students collect three-dimensional objects and use them to inspire writing. This activity can be tied to a classroom unit of study or can just be used to address the bigger question...Where did it come from?

Topics:

1. Nature's Artifacts:
   - types of rocks
   - shell types
   - leaf types
   - bones

2. Science Riddles
   - Guess what it is.
   - Where did I find it?

3. Counting Books for Math Practice
   1 leaf, 2 rocks, 3 bones, etc.

Basic Steps to Follow

Materials:

- a small box with a removable lid (checkbook boxes are perfect)
- construction paper or shelf paper cut to match the width of the box (make it as long as your stories require)
- sheets of writing paper cut to match the length and width of the box
- scissors
- glue
- pencils and felt pens
- a collection of found objects: rocks, leaves, bottle tops, bones, buttons, pine cones, seed pods, etc.

Directions:

1. Students collect the items that are the topic of this book.

2. Accordion fold the construction or shelf paper (precut to fit the length of the box) to match the width of the box. How many writing sections did you get?

3. Plan the story or riddle to fit that number of sections. Provide one sheet of writing paper (cut to size) for each section of the accordion-folded paper. Students write out their story or riddle on the writing paper.

4. When the writing is complete, glue the pages to the folded paper.

5. Glue whatever artifacts the students are using to the folded paper.

6. Glue the bottom surface of the last fold to the inside base of the box.

7. Cut a piece of construction paper the size of the box top on which to write the title of the story. Glue it to lid of the box.

8. Put the lid on the box. Share the story with a friend.

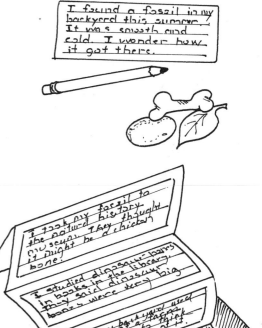

Magnets

A File Folder Book

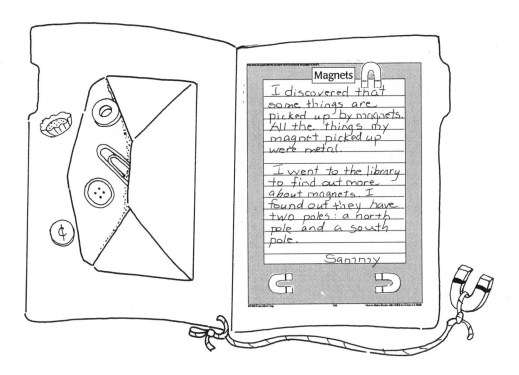

Project:

This science experiment report gives students an opportunity to interact with scientific concepts. Students will gather information, experiment with what magnets attract and then summarize results. This folder may be placed in a center to share with other students.

Topics:

1. What items are attracted by magnets?

2. What items are not attracted by magnets?

3. How do magnets work?

4. What diffent kinds of magnets are there?

5. What is the difference between a permanent magnet and an electromagnet?

Facts about magnets:

Magnets have two poles: a north pole and a south pole.
- Unlike poles attract.
- Like poles repel.

There are two basic types of magnets:
- *Permanent magnets* attract all the time.
- *Electromagnets* only attract when turned on electronically.

Magnets only stick to four metals: iron, nickel cobalt and steel (a combination of metals including iron). Any object made of these metals may be magnetized.

Basic Steps to Follow

Materials:

- letter size file folder
- envelope
- writing form on page 108
- yarn
- a magnet
- a collection of small items that may or may not be attracted to a magnet
- hole punch, scissors, felt pens and pencils

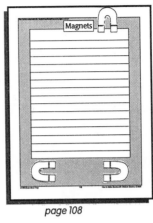

page 108

Directions:

1. Provide each student with a magnet and an envelope full of assorted items to test with the magnet.

2. Establish the writing guidelines:
   - what to record
   - where to record it
   - amount of time available

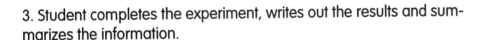

3. Student completes the experiment, writes out the results and summarizes the information.

4. The experiment report is pasted into a file folder along with the envelope of items tested.

5. The magnet is attached to the folder with a strip of yarn.

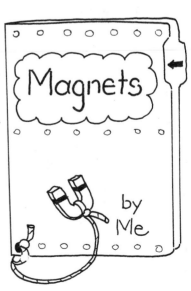

6. The front of the file folder may be decorated with felt pens. The cover is acting as the title page and therefore should list the author, illustrator, date of experiment, and the title of this report.

7. Set older students to investigating how magnets work. This may be done by individual students or in cooperative-learning groups. Provide needed resource materials.

Encyclopedia of Prehistoric Animals

A Binder Resource Book

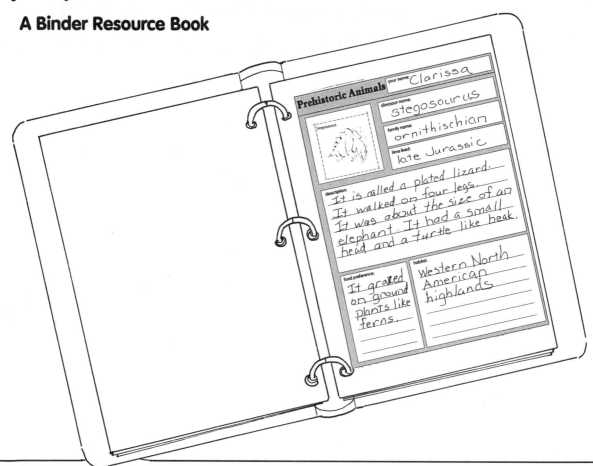

The handwritten report page reads:

Prehistoric Animals

Your name: Clarissa
dinosaur name: stegosaurus
family name: ornithischian
time lived: late Jurassic

description: It is called a plated lizard. It walked on four legs. It was about the size of an elephant. It had a small head and a turtle like beak.

food preference: It grazed on ground plants like ferns.

habitat: Western North American highlands

Project:

This class project presents student reports on prehistoric animals in a useful and informative way. Each student reports on a different dinosaur. The reports are placed alphabetically in a binder to create an encyclopedia. The class provides a title page, a table of contents, a date of publication and a front cover.

Topics:

1. Individual Prehistoric Animals
   - their sizes and family ties
   - their habitats
   - their food preferences
   - the time frame when they lived
   - interesting facts about this dinosaur

2. A timeline of the dinosaur age and the different types that evolved in each period.

3. Write a fictional story incorporating the scientific facts about these giants.

4. Use the height and weight information to create a book about sizes.

Dinosaurs and other prehistoric animals are extinct and known only through fossils. Scientists who study the fossils are called *paleontologists*.

Dinosaurs were:
- not all big.
- not all fierce.
- not all meat eaters.
- not all shaped the same.
- reptiles but some looked like birds or other animals.
- alive during the Triasic, Jurassic and Cretaceous eras.

Basic Steps to Follow

Materials:

- a report form for each student on page 109
- copies of the dinosaur picture forms on pages 110 and 111
- a 3-hole binder
- hole punch, scissors, felt pens and pencils
- paper for title page, table of contents, etc.
- construction paper to use as a front

pages 109-111

Directions:

1. Share books about prehistoric animals with students. Each student picks an animal to study. Make a list of each one chosen so that as many of the letters of the alphabet as possible are represented.

2. Students do research on their chosen animal and complete the report form.

3. The reports are shared with a friend who acts as an editor. Spelling and grammar corrections are made. The report is copied on a new form and a picture is added.

4. The reports are arranged alphabetically.

5. A table of contents is prepared by a committee.

6. A front cover and a title page are designed.

7. Older students may also prepare a glossary of terms for reference.

All Kinds of Weather

A Pull-Tab Book

Tanya

Hail

Hunks of ice fell from the sky. They hit the ground hard and bounced. These hailstones soon melted. Hailstones start as raindrops. The rain drops are frozen and blown about by the wind.

Project:

Each student investigates a different type of weather and how it happens. These individual student projects are collected together and made into a class book.

Topics:

•Write a weather report using these terms:

rain	wind
snow	lightning
sleet	thunder
hail	sunshine
clouds	hurricanes
fog	tornadoes

• Create a weather quiz: What type of weather is hiding under the tab?

• Explain how a weather satellite helps us today.

Earth is surrounded by a blanket of gases. These gases form our *atmosphere*. The atmosphere keeps us from burning up in the heat of the day and from freezing in the cold of night.

The lowest level of the atmosphere is called the *troposphere*. It is where the movement and changes we call weather happen. As parts of the Earth cool off or heat up, you can see changes happen. Warm air rises and cold air moves in. We feel this movement as wind. There is another change that happens. Water evaporates and condenses. This causes us to have rain and snow.

Basic Steps to Follow

Materials:
- basic writing form and pull tab pattern on pages 112 and 113
- scissors, felt pens or crayons and pencils
- 9"x12" (23 x 30 cm) sheets of construction paper
- paper fasteners
- a glue stick
- reference materials on the topic of weather
- 2 sheets (same size as construction paper) of yellow tagboard for a cover

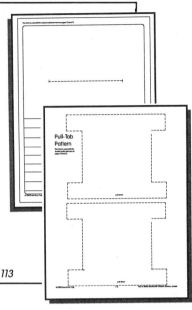

pages 112 and 113

Directions:

1. Read about different types of weather forms. Let each student pick a form. Students should gather information on their form and write a paragraph summarizing what they have learned. The paragraph should be edited by a friend before being copied on the final form.

2. Assemble the writing form and the pull tab.
Slit on the dotted line. Cut out the pull tab and insert through the slit.

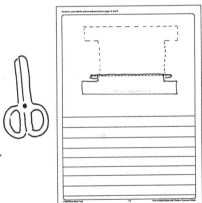

3. The pulltab is pulled down and the type of weather is illustrated on the tab. Now it can be pulled down or pushed back behind the cloud. Students may add other details to their illustrations.

4. The form is glued onto a sheet of construction paper. Glue stick should be applied carefully to the outside edges of the paper. Caution should be taken not to allow glue to interfere with the pull-tab mechanism.

5. The finished forms may then be placed in a class book. Select students to provide a table of contents and a title page.

6. Hinge the tagboard cover. See page 3 for directions.

7. Illustrate the cover with felt pens or torn paper. Place the finished forms inside. Secure with paper fasteners.

My Very Own Book About

Day and Night

A Pop-Up Book

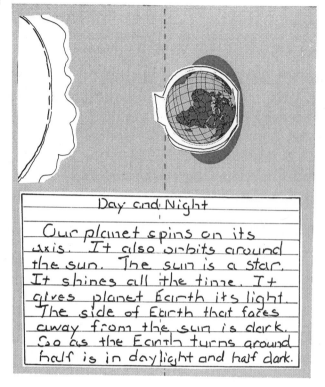

Day and Night

Our planet spins on its axis. It also orbits around the sun. The sun is a star. It shines all the time. It gives planet Earth its light. The side of Earth that faces away from the sun is dark. So as the Earth turns around half is in daylight and half dark.

Project:

Each student has the opportunity to show how night and day happen on the planet Earth. Provide students with reference materials and discuss the topic as a class.

Topics:

1. What causes daylight?

2. What causes night?

3. How does the Earth's movement cause night and day?

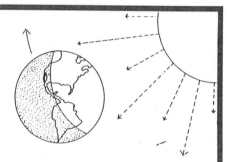

The sun is a star that shines all the time. The Earth is a planet that moves around the sun. The Earth also revolves on an axis. It spins all the way around in 24 hours. As it spins, we have sunrise, daylight, sunset and night.

Basic Steps to Follow

Materials:

- a 12" x 18" (30 x 46 cm) sheet of dark blue construction paper per student
- writing paper
- a globe form on page 114
- a small sheet of yellow construction paper per child
- crayons
- scissors
- pencils
- paste

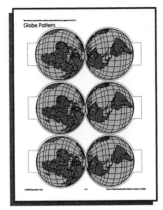

page 114

Directions:

1. Create the pop-up globe first.
   a. Students cut out the globe pattern and fold it on the dotted lines.
   b. They should color both sides of the globe. One side should be colored as if it were experiencing daylight and the other side should be dark to represent the night.

2. Cut a section of sun from the yellow paper. Paste it on the left side of the construction paper.

3. Fold the blue paper in half the long way.

4. Paste the globe pattern into the center fold. Now the student must demonstrate an understanding of the concept being taught here. Which side of the globe will face the sun and which side will face away?

5. Students write an explanation of how night and day occur. Their work is checked by a student editor and then recopied on another sheet of paper. The finished copy is then pasted on the large construction paper below the sun and the globe.

6. Students close their book and use the left-over yellow scraps of construction paper to make a front cover. They sign the book as the author. Now they are ready to take it home to share what they have learned with family and friends.

                   How to Make Books with Children-Science & Math

Electricity
A Flap Book

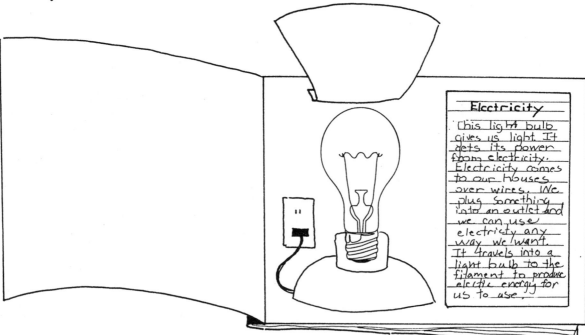

Electricity

This light bulb gives us light. It gets its power from electricity. Electricity comes to our houses over wires. We plug something into an outlet and we can use electricty any way we want. It travels into a light bulb to the filament to produce electric energy for us to use.

Project:

Read about current and static electricity. Now let students put what they have learned to work in this class book.

Topics:

1. What is electricity?

2. Where does electricity come from?

3. Is there more than one kind of electricity?

4. How does a light bulb make use of electricity?

5. How do light bulbs differ?

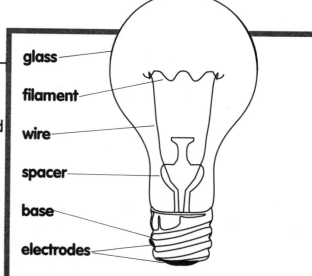

glass

filament

wire

spacer

base

electrodes

Electricity gives us power from tiny particles called electrons. When electrons flow, we call it *current electricity*. When electrons collect in one place, we call it *static electricity*.

When electricity is conducted to a bulb, it gives us light. The electricity enters through the electrodes and the wires carry it to and from the filament. The glass protects the wires and the base fits into the socket of the lamp.

How to Make Books with Children-Science & Math

Basic Steps to Follow

Materials:

- bulb and shade pattern on page 115
- 9" x 12" (23 x 30 cm) white construction paper
- writing paper
- tagboard for front and back covers
- paste
- stapler
- scissors
- pencils
- crayons or felt pens
- reference books on the topic of electricity

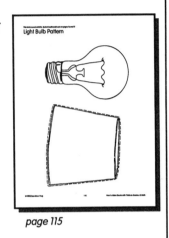

page 115

Directions:

1. Cut out the pattern pieces.

2. Lay the bulb on the construction paper.

3. A light fixture is drawn on the paper to fit with the light bulb. The bulb is pasted in place.

4. The lamp shade is pasted as a flap over the light bulb.

5. Students complete a rough draft on the topic. After it is proofed and corrected, it is copied on the writing form.

6. All student pages are assembled together. A hinged cover is made from the tagboard. See page 3 for directions.

7. Staple the front and back covers and the stories together in the left margin.

What Is a Mushroom?

A Shape Book

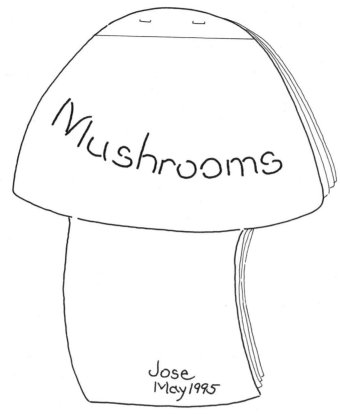

Mushrooms

Jose
May 1995

Project:

This book provides students an opportunity to learn about what a fungus is and what it does. Reference books and encyclopedias can help students discover the facts about this class of living organisms. This fascinating area of study can motivate students to view their world in a new way.

Topics:

1. What is a mushroom and how does it grow?

2. How many different mushrooms can you name?

3. Are mushrooms a good source of food?

4. What other fungi share our world?

5. What is the difference between a mushroom and a toadstool?

6. Are some mushrooms poisonous?

7. Discuss the life cycle of a mushroom.

Mushrooms:
- are a type of plant called *fungi*.
- never bloom.
- are fast growing.
- grow in moist places.
- are sometimes good to eat but some types are poisonous.
- grow from *spores*, not from seeds.
- come in many sizes, shapes and colors.

 How to Make Books with Children-Science & Math

Basic Steps to Follow

Materials:

- 2 sheets of 9" x 12" (23 x 30 cm) brown construction paper per child
- writing paper
- crayons or felt pens
- pencils
- scissors
- stapler
- reference books on mushrooms

Directions:

1. Students research their "mushroom" questions. They write out a rough draft of their report. An editor friend checks for clarity and spelling.

2. A cover is created for this book from two sheets of brown construction paper. The student lightly sketches the mushroom with a pencil before cutting out the mushroom shape. Both pieces of paper may be cut at the same time.

3. Details are added to the cover with black crayon.

4. Writing paper is cut in the same shape. Trace the outline with a pencil before cutting out the shape. Cut as many sheets of paper as the report requires.

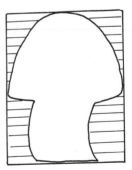

5. Copy the report on the mushroom-shaped paper. Add illustrations where needed.

6. Staple the report inside the cover along the top of the mushroom.

What's the Matter?
A Shape Book

Project:

This book provides an opportunity for students to write on what they have learned about the changing states of matter. They will discuss how matter changes by freezing or melting. Students may then place these projects together in a colorful cover to share with others.

Topics:

• Explain what happens when a solid melts.

• Explain what happens when a liquid freezes.

• Write a fictional story entitled "What's the Matter?" Explain to the melting snowman what is happening as he melts. He may be changing, but he is still made of the same stuff; just in a different form.

Matter is the material that things are made of. Matter has weight, occupies space and exists as a solid, a liquid or a gas.

Solid - a substance whose particles (atoms or molecules) don't wiggle much and stay in place.

Liquid - a substance whose particles wiggle more, spread out, and start changing places as they flow.

Gas - a substance whose particles can expand without limit.

Basic Steps to Follow

Materials:

- 9" x 12" (23 x 30 cm) blue construction paper
  (1 sheet for each student)
  (2 sheets to use as a cover)
- snowman pattern on page 116
- paste
- scissors
- felt pens or crayons
- stapler

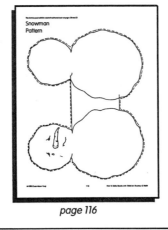

page 116

Directions:

Student Pages
1. Students cut out the snowman pattern.
2. The writing form is used to explain what is happening to the snowman as he melts.
3. Fold the pattern in half and draw a snowman on the front.
4. Paste this snowman to the blue construction paper.
5. Create a background with crayon or cut paper.

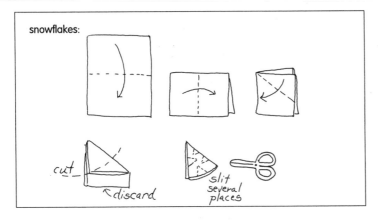

Book Cover
1. Collect student pages and add a front and back cover.
2. Print the title on the front cover.
3. Decorate the cover with tiny snowflakes cut by the contributing authors. They each put their name on one of the flakes.

4. Staple the book together in the left margin.

Guess the Question
How Sound Travels
A Quiz Book on Sound

The question.....
How does sound move
through the air from
you to your friend?

vibration

Project:

This books gives your students the chance to investigate how sound travels. After reading and discussing the basic facts of how vibrations travel through space, each student may create a riddle book where the answer is given and the challenge to the reader is to figure out the question.

Topics:

Quiz questions that students might investigate:

1. What is sound?

2. How does it travel?

3. Why don't we hear sounds from space?

4. Faster vibrations make higher sounds.

5. Bigger vibrations make louder sounds.

• Sound is caused by wave-like vibrations of molecules. If there are no molecules, sound can't get through. The closer together the molecules, the better sound is conducted. Human ears are designed to hear sounds carried by air.

• Sound vibrations look like waves.

-a high-pitched sound

-a lower sound

-a LOUD high sound

Basic Steps to Follow

Materials:

- 12" x 18" (30 x 46 cm) construction paper
- reproducible form on page 117
- string
- hole punch
- hole reinforcers (optional)
- crayons or felt pens
- pencil
- three-hole punch
- binder

page 117

Directions:

1. Students choose a scientific question relating to how sound travels and research the answer. The answer is written on the speech bubble and the question is written on the reproducible form.

2. The construction paper is folded so that the two ends meet in the middle. The question form is pasted inside the lower portion.

3. The two characters are colored, cut out and pasted to the construction paper.

4. Holes are punched as indicated on each character.

5. A strip of 24" (61 cm) string is cut and slipped through the two holes.

6. The speech bubble is cut out, a hole is punched to slip the string through. The two ends of the string are tied together on the backside.

7. Slip the bubble from the mouth of the character on the left to the ear of the character on the right.

8. Three-hole punch the riddles across the top. Place all student riddles together in a binder. Create a cover for the front of the binder.

Phases of the Moon

Unfolding Book

The Phases

The moon circles around the Earth. It takes 28 days to get around. As it goes it looks like its shape changes. It really doesn't. It happens that way because it reflects the sun's light. It tricks us!

Project:

Students write short reports about the phases of the moon. Bind the students' reports together into a class book. Invite one of the students to create a cover for the book. Future students may want to use this book for reference. Students must double-check their facts because they are creating a reference book for others to use.

Topics:

1. As the moon goes around the Earth, it looks different to us. We call these *phases*.
It takes 28 days for the moon to go around the Earth. During that time there will be one full moon and one new moon. The other phases will occur twice each; once on the way from full to new, and again on the way back on the other side.

2. How do the relative positions of the sun, Earth, and moon create the moon phases?

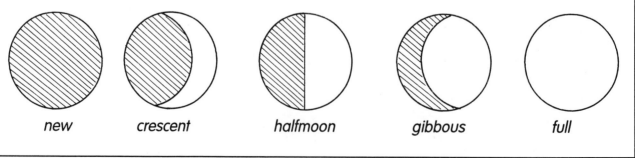

new   *crescent*   *halfmoon*   *gibbous*   *full*

Basic Steps to Follow

Materials:

- 8 1/2" x 11" (22 x 28 cm) unlined paper
- 9" x 12" (23 x 30 cm) dark blue construction paper
- writing paper
- crayons
- scissors
- paste or glue

Directions:

Unfolding Paper
1. Fold the unlined paper into sixths.
2. Cut out the lower center section.
3. Label and draw the moons in the sections.
4. Refold the paper beginning with the right-hand lower box.
5. Roll the paper up again. Glue it to the upper right-hand corner of the blue construction paper.

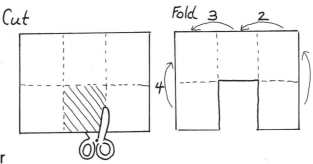

The Report
1. Gather information from encyclopedias and non-fiction books.
Write a paragraph that explains why the moon appears to have different phases.
2. Edit this report with a friend, make corrections, and copy the report on the final writing paper. Glue this paper to the lower half of the blue construction paper.
3. Add the planet Earth and the sun with crayon.

The Book
1. Collect all the reports and add a tagboard front and back cover to the book. Hinge the front cover. See page 3 for directions.
2. Put a title page in the front.

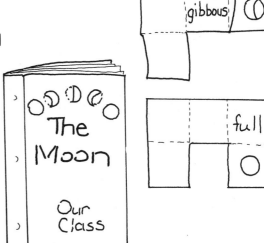

Our Book of Science Questions

Unrolling Book

Question:
How does electricity get to my lamp in the livingroom?

1 Water or air turns a propeller.

2 The propeller turns a generator to make electricity.

3 Wires carry electricity into your house. First a transformer sets the strength just right.

4 We turn the switch on the light and electricity is there!

Project:

This open-ended type of student-authored book allows for individual variations in interest and abilities. The teacher conducts a brainstorming session to list possible questions. Then students must develop a four-part explanation to answer the question.

Topics:

1. How does electricity get to my house?

2. How does sound travel?

3. Where does rain come from?

4. How do fish breathe under water?

5. Why can an airplane fly?

6. What makes a motor run?

7. How does an escalator work?

8. How do we get water in our houses?

9. How does blood get around to parts of my body?

10. How do telephones work?

Basic Steps to Follow

Materials:

- 8 1/2" x 11" (22 x 28 cm) white construction paper
- writing form on page 118
- scissors
- pencil
- felt pens
- paste or glue
- tape

page 118

Directions:

1. Students choose the question they will study.

2. After researching the question, the students use the writing form to develop the step-by-step explanation.

3. Each student cuts one sheet of the construction paper down the center and tapes the ends together.

4. They fold the strip in half and then fold it into thirds.

5. Open the strip and refold beginning on the right side.

6. Cut apart the boxes on the writing form. Paste the boxes to the folded construction paper.

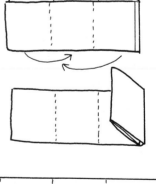

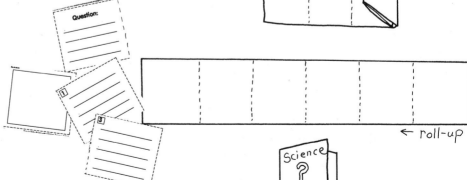

← roll-up

Dictionary of Science Vocabulary
A Book on a Ring

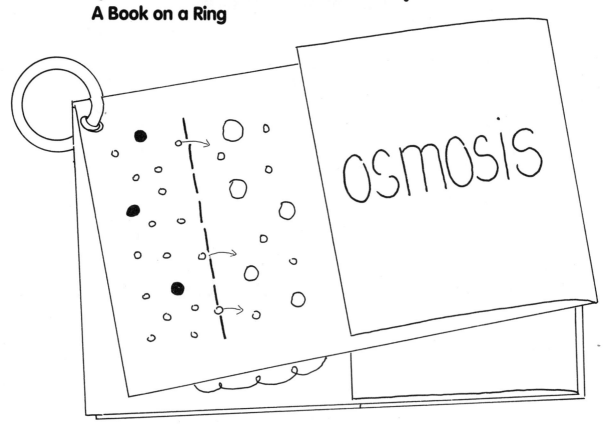

Project:

Use this project to reinforce vocabulary development in any area of science students are studying. Each student researches the meaning of a separate term and develops a definition. The sheets are all placed in alphabetical order so that other students can find definitions when they need them.

Topics:

1. Weather Vocabulary
   sunny, stormy, hail, sleet, snow, rain,
   turbulent, hurricane, tornado, cumulus

2. Mammals
   Give three facts about each animal.

3. Parts of the Body

4. Geological Terms-Features of the Earth

5. Objects in Space

6. Plant Terms

 How to Make Books with Children-Science & Math

Basic Steps to Follow

Materials:

- 4 1/2" x 12" (11 x 30 cm) white construction paper for inside pages
- colored construction paper for the cover
- pencil
- felt tip pens
- scissors
- hole punch
- 1" (2.5 cm) binder ring
- ruler

Directions:

Beginning

Brainstorm the vocabulary for a science unit and list it on the board. Let each student pick a term and write a definition. Share the definitions and decide if they are clear and concise.

Inside Pages

1. Fold over 4" (10 cm) on one end of the long white paper.

2. Set the paper up in the following format:

   Write the word on the flap.
   Illustrate.
   Write the definition under the flap.

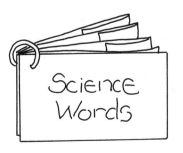

The Cover

1. Collect papers. Put them in **alphabetical** order.

2. Design a cover sheet that lists the title and the authors. Cut the paper to the same size as the definition sheets. (Remember one side was folded over.)

3. Punch a hole in the upper left-hand corner of all pages. Insert the ring through the hole.

4. Share the book with other students.

         How to Make Books with Children-Science & Math

Cycles
Pop-Up Book

Tadpoles
When the eggs hatch, the pond is full of tadpoles. They wiggle and swim fast.

Project:

What cycles do you want your students to investigate? This little book gives them four inside pop-up pages to illustrate any life or seasonal cycles that you may be studying. The writing area is limited but they will have enough room to discuss basic facts. The illustration will also require knowledge of the subject.

Topics:

1. The Four Seasons - illustrate the same landscape in four different seasons.

2. Animal Life Cycles
    a frog -egg, tadpole, tadpole with legs, land-living frog
    a butterfly - egg, caterpillar, chrysalis, butterfly
    a bird - egg, little wet bird, bird in nest, full grown bird

3. The Growth Cycle of a Plant
    seed
    sprout
    seedling
    mature plant with flowers

Basic Steps to Follow

Materials:

- 9" x 12" (23 x 30 cm) white construction paper (4 per student)
- 9" x 12" (23 x 30 cm) colored construction paper (1 per student)
- plain paper for the rough draft
- writing paper cut to 4" x 8" (10 x 20 cm)
- a box of construction paper scraps or small sheets of paper in assorted colors
- crayons or felt pens
- pencils
- scissors
- glue

Directions:

1. After students have chosen their topic, they map out 4 parts to their story on the rough draft paper. They write a paragraph in each section and make a sketch of what they want to show in their pop-up illustrations.

2. Prepare the pop-up pages:

fold and cut	bend forward and back	push through

Repeat this process on all 4 of the white construction paper sheets.

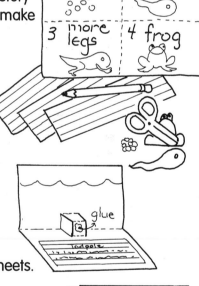

3. Have students copy their edited rough drafts on the writing paper sheets. Glue them below the pop-up tabs.

4. How will the illustration be done? Color the background behind the pop-up tab. Cut out paper figures to glue to the face of the pop-up tabs. These characters stand away from the background as you open the book.

5. Glue the pages back-to-back.

6. Fold the colored construction paper in half. Place glue on the inside, around the perimeter of the paper. Wrap it around the pop-up pages. Cut out paper scraps to decorate the cover. Print the title of the book and the name of the author.

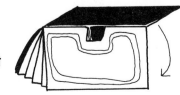

A Study of Mold
The Lunch Bag Surprise
A Book Made of Bags

Project:

Discuss what mold is. Set up classroom experiments so that students can watch mold grow. Let students create bag books that illustrate the characteristics of mold as it grows on a variety of foods.

Topics:

1. What is growing in my lunch bag?

2. Nature's Way of Recycling

Mold is a type of fungus that grows on live matter. It grows best with warm temperatures, some moisture and darkness.

Conduct several experiments in the classroom showing how mold grows, what it looks like on different materials and how far it can progress. It works well to place slices or pieces of food in small plastic food containers. Cover the container with plastic wrap with holes punched in it (you don't want students to breathe in the spores).

How to Make Books with Children-Science & Math

Basic Steps to Follow

Materials:

- a brown lunch bag for each student
- a copy of the writing form on page 119
- crayons or felt pens
- paste
- pencil
- stapler

Optional
- gray tempera paint and sponges
- cotton
- construction paper scraps

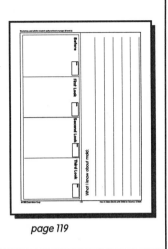

page 119

Directions:

1. Conduct classroom experiments with fungi so that students have real life experiences on which to report.

2. Provide each student with a brown bag and the reproducible writing form. They are to pretend that they have forgotton part of their lunch at school and they are going to describe what they then discover growing on this food.

3. Students are to fold the writing form in half.
They draw or cut from construction paper scraps the food they "have forgotten" and left in their lunch bag. They make this item four times–once in each of the four boxes. Then they show what happens as mold grows on this food. They may:
- illustrate with crayons.
- pull cotton balls apart and glue it onto the food showing the progressive changes.
- use gray tempera paint sponged on to give the effect.

On the other side of this form, students write about how and why this change is taking place.

4. When each sheet is complete, students slip them into the lunch bags and write their names on the front.

5. The bags are collected and another bag is placed on top to act as a cover. Staple the bags together on the left side being careful not to staple any of the stories inside the bags.

Our Five Senses
An Individual Pop-Up Book

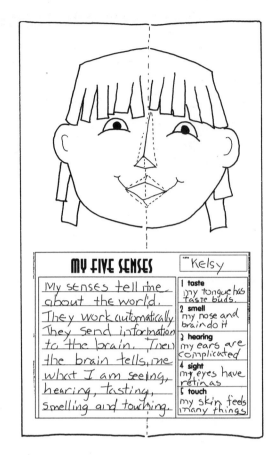

Project:

This pop-up book offers students a challenging way to share what they have learned about how we learn about our world. Each student will have his/her own book to share with family and friends.

Topics:

1. Our Five Senses - Discuss how these five senses serve us. List the types of information that we gather with each of these senses.
- taste
- smell
- touch
- hearing
- sight

2. How My Body Works
Take each sense and develop a scientific description for how it works.
For example:
- *Show how the eyelids protect the eye.*
- *Discuss how the lashes keep dust out of the eye.*
- *Do a diagram that shows how the optic nerve carries message to the brain.*

Basic Steps to Follow

Materials:

- 12" x 18" (30 x 46 cm) construction paper for the covers
- copies of the reproducible writing page and the pop-up form on pages 120 and 121
- a selection of extra construction paper to use in adding details
- crayons or felt pens
- pencils
- scissors
- paste

pages 120 and 121

Directions:

The Pop-Up Form

1. Students make the pop-up pattern:

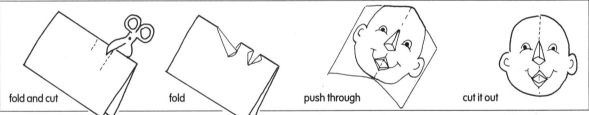

fold and cut   fold   push through   cut it out

2. Color this form.

The Writing Form

1. Students prepare a rough draft of their report.

2. The final copy is written on the writing form.

The Book

1. Students take their construction paper sheets and fold them in half vertically.

2. The pop-up form is pasted on the top portion. What creative additions can students add to this picture? They may cut out and add hair, a neck and shoulders or earrings.

3. The writing form is pasted on the bottom portion.

4. The paper is pressed closed. A cover design is created with felt pens, crayons, or collage.

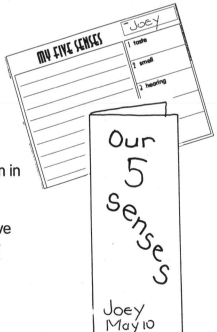

Scientific Opposites

A Two-Tab Pop-Up

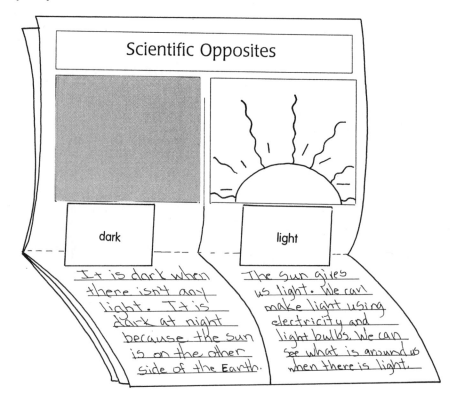

Scientific Opposites

dark

light

It is dark when there isn't any light. It is dark at night because the sun is on the other side of the Earth.

The sun gives us light. We can make light using electricity and light bulbs. We can see what is around us when there is light.

Project:

Create a group book illustrating a collection of scientific opposites. Creating pop-up books is an enjoyable way to expand scientific vocabulary and concepts.

Topics:

This project is enriched by a search in the science section of the library. Let students browse and collect ideas and then brainstorm to share what they have discovered. Add to the list other concepts you want to emphasize:

Sink - Float

Sound - Silence

Dark - Light

Evaporation - Condensation

Gravity - Weightlessness

Wet- Dry

Basic Steps to Follow

Materials:

- the writing pop-up form on page 122
- copies of the opposite cards on page 123
- 1 sheet of 9" x 12" (23 x 30 cm) construction paper for a cover
- crayons or felt pens
- pencil
- scissors
- glue

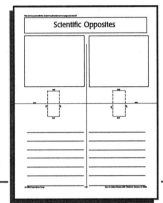

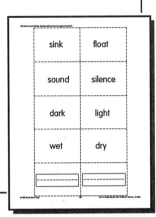

pages 122 and 123

sink	float
sound	silence
dark	light
wet	dry

Directions:

1. Each student chooses a set of opposites to write about. They may read about the topic to gather information and facts. Students summarize what they have learned in one paragraph on each of the opposites. They prepare a rough draft, have it edited, and then copy it on the writing form.

2. A picture is drawn to illustrate each of the concepts.

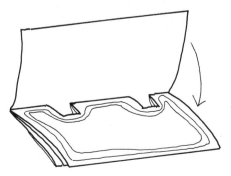

3. Prepare the pop-up:

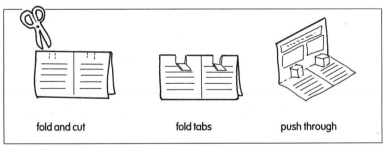

fold and cut   fold tabs   push through

4. Glue the appropriate topics to the front of each of the two tabs. Place glue only on the front of the tab.

5. Glue the students' papers back-to-back to bind it into a book.

6. Wrap the construction paper sheet around the book. Glue it in place. Decorate the cover.

Animal Homes

A Layered Book

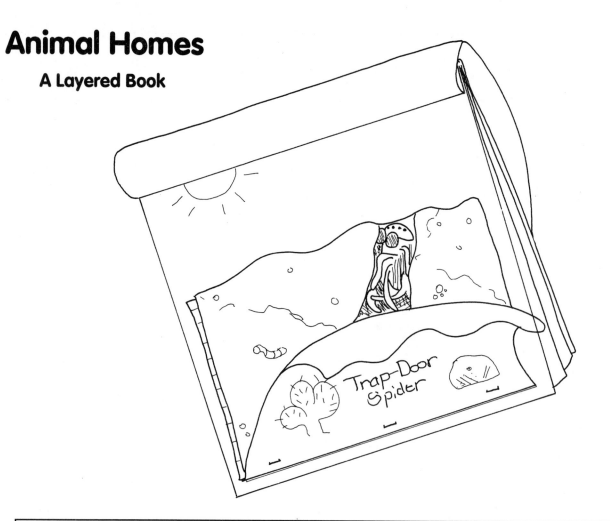

Trap-Door Spider

Project:
This project challenges students to develop a cross-section of an animal's home. This layered book concept allows students to take a peek inside these homes and discuss how they are built and what functions they specifically serve.

Topics:

The Trap-Door Spider

The Beaver Lodge

The Bee Hive

The Wolf's Den

The Bear's Cave

The Bird's Nest

The Gopher's Hole

The Ants' Hill

Basic Steps to Follow

Materials:

- 2 pieces of 9" x 12" (23 x 30 cm) white art paper per child
- 1 sheet of 9" x 12" (23 x 30 cm) writing paper per child
- 1 sheet of 12" x 12" (30 x 30 cm) colored construction paper per child and an extra sheet to use as a cover
- paper fasteners
- crayons or felt pens
- scissors
- stapler

Directions:

1. Sketch the animal's home on one sheet of the white paper.

2. Put the 2 pieces of white paper and the writing paper together. Cut out the picture of the home. Now you will have 3 pieces of paper cut in the same shape. (Cut more sheets of lined paper if more writing space is needed.)

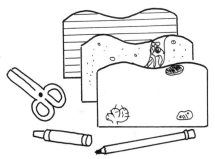

3. Draw the animal inside its home.

4. Write about the animal on the last sheet of paper. List as many facts as possible about how this home is built, how long it is usually used and how the animal maintains this home.

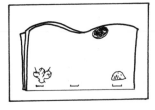

5. Lay all three pages on the construction paper. Staple them along the bottom.

6. Gather all the students' stories together and design a cover for the book. Bind them across the top by inserting two or three paper fasteners.

Why Does It Fly?

An Expanding Book

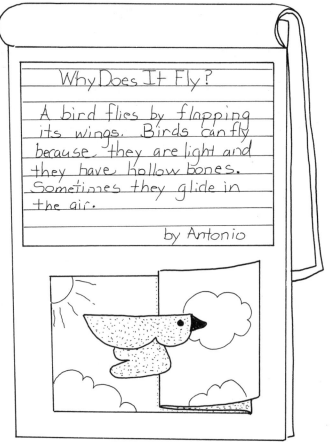

Why Does It Fly?

A bird flies by flapping its wings. Birds can fly because they are light and they have hollow bones. Sometimes they glide in the air.

by Antonio

Project:

How can birds fly? How can jets, helicopters and rockets zoom through the sky? After researching the principles of flight, make a book to reinforce what is learned. Include information on all different types of objects that can achieve flight in this student-authored book.

Topics:

1. Birds - Investigate the physiological features that make birds capable of flight.

2. Airplanes - Examine the history of flight from 1903 and the Wright brothers til modern-day jets and super jets.

3. Helicopters - What unique features of this vehicle have made it an important part of our transportation system? Why is it valuable in responding to emergencies?

4. Rockets - What ever made man think he could soar into outer space? Approach this question in two different ways: *historical* dates and events and *scientific* facts about rockets and how they fly.

5. Balloons - What is helium and why does it lift a balloon up and away?

Basic Steps to Follow

Materials:

- 6" x 18" (15 x 46 cm) white construction paper (1 per student)
- 9" x 12" (23 x 30 cm) writing paper (1 per student)
- 12" x 18" (30 x 46 cm) colored construction paper (1 per student and one extra for a cover)
- 3" x 5" (8 x 13 cm) file cards (1 per student)
- paper fasteners
- crayons
- pencil
- scissors
- paste

Directions:

1. Collect nonfiction books on flight. Let students pick different objects to focus on: jets, props, rockets, etc. They will prepare a rough draft on their topic, share it with an editor and then complete a final copy on the writing paper.

2. Fold the long white construction paper.

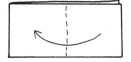

3. Use crayons to create a blue skyscape with white clouds on the white paper. Cover the entire sheet.

4. Sketch and then color and cut out the topic object on the file card.

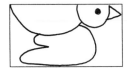  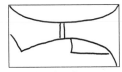  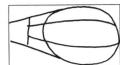

5. Paste the right edge of the card to the folded edge. Now you can pull the right-hand side of the paper and the page will expand out and the object appears to shoot up and away.

6. Paste the back of the skyscape and the writing paper to the large construction paper.

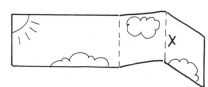

7. Collect all students' reports and add a cover. Decorate the cover with samples of all the topics covered in the reports. Bind the pages together along the top edge. Hold the pages together with paper fasteners.

The Rainforest

A Flip Book

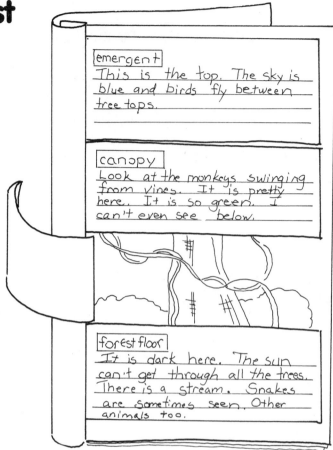

emergent
This is the top. The sky is blue and birds fly between tree tops.

canopy
Look at the monkeys swinging from vines. It is pretty here. It is so green. I can't even see below.

forest floor
It is dark here. The sun can't get through all the trees. There is a stream. Snakes are sometimes seen. Other animals too.

Project:

This book encourages students to become aware of the special features that are typical of the various levels of the rainforest.

Topics:

The Rainforest Has Layers

Animals in the Rainforest

Plants in the Rainforest

The trees in the Rainforest are so tall they seem to touch the sky and block out most of the sunlight. Eight-inch (20.5 cm) butterflies float through the air and beetles as big as baseballs crawl on the ground. The air is damp and small frogs can be seen sitting on leaves. The howler monkeys and scarlet macaws can be seen in the branches. Life in the rainforest exists at different levels or layers. Each of these layers has a special name:

- *emergent* - The top layer includes the tips of the trees as the tall ones extend above the canopy.
- *canopy* - Monkeys, apes, sloths, and exotic plants live here. The canopy is like a big green umbrella.
- *understory* - Bushes, large green plants and small trees make up this layer. Lizards, bats, frogs, and butterflies are a few of the animals that live here.
- *forest floor* - This is the ground level. Snakes, tapirs and fungi are a few of the species that live here. It is dark on the floor because the trees keep out most of the light.

     How to Make Books with Children-Science & Math

Basic Steps to Follow

Materials:

- a 12" x 18" (30 x 46 cm) sheet of green construction paper for a cover
- 2 sheets of copy paper for each student
- 2 copies of the writing form on page 124 for each student
- crayons, felt pens
- pencil
- stapler
- scissors
- a collection of leaves (optional)

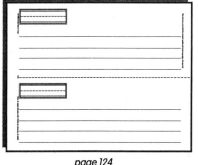

page 124

Directions:

Individual Pages

1. Read about the layers of the rainforest. Each student develops a paragraph for each layer. After the rough draft has been corrected, the students copy the information on the writing form. (Students will need two copies of the form.)

2. Place one sheet of copy paper behind each writing form. Cut on the dotted line. Staple the paper to the large construction paper.

3. Begin at the bottom and lift up one section at a time. Lightly sketch with a pencil. When the picture is complete, all layers of the rainforest will be visible. When the sketch is complete the student lifts all the layers and uses crayon or felt pen to color the entire picture. Encourage students to use rich bold color to match the lush growth found in this habitat.

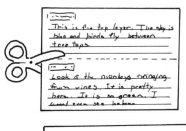

The Cover

Set out a collection of leaves and broken crayons (without paper covers). Students create leaf rubbings on their sheet of green construction paper by placing the paper over the leaves and rubbing with the side of the crayon. Staple the pages together along the left-hand side.

Our Seed Catalog

A Binder Book

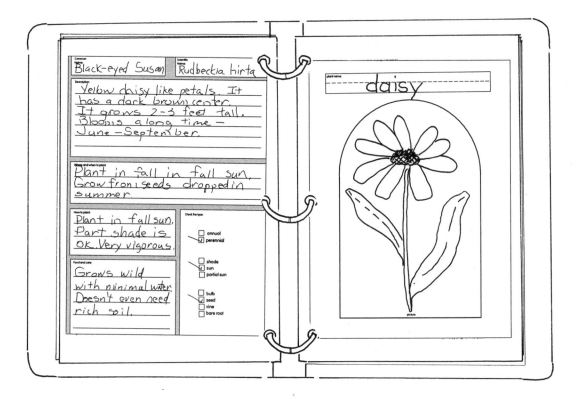

Project:

Let's involve students in the study of specific plants and how they grow. They will be gathering information and recording it. When all student reports are finished, provide time to compare and contrast the different varieties of plants studied.

Topics:

Students will each pick a different plant. They will locate an actual seed of this plant, a picture of the mature plant, and they will complete the information requested on the form.

Plant categories to choose from:
- plants with flowers
- perennials
- annuals
- deciduous
- a fruit-producing plant
- a vegetable-producing plant
- a cone-producing plant

Basic Steps to Follow

Materials:

- a copy of the forms on pages 125 and 126 for each student in the group
- crayons or felt pens
- a pencil
- hole punch
- a 3 ring binder
- glue
- an assortment of garden and plant reference books
- actual seed packets from the nursery

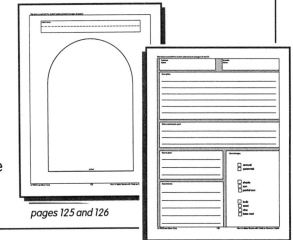

pages 125 and 126

Directions:

1. Students pick the variety of plant they want to study. They locate information on the plant.

2. They draw a picture of the mature plant on the front of the form and letter its name across the top.

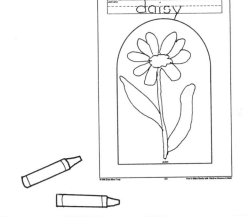

3. Students record specific facts about the plant on their information sheet.

4. Glue the two forms back-to-back.

5. Three-hole punch the papers so they will fit in the binder.

6. Collect all student forms and arrange them in the binder in alphabetical order.

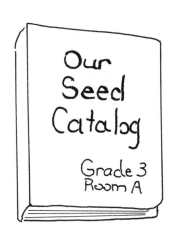

Our Seed Catalog

Grade 3 Room A

7. Title the binder **Our Seed Catalog**. Keep it as a reference book in the classroom library.

Camouflage Riddles

A Flap-Peek Book

Who hides under the bushes and croaks at our dog?

by Perry

Project:

This project will motivate research and study about animals and how they survive in the wild. Camouflage is one of the adaptations that nature has provided to protect animals from their predators.

Topics:

1. What interesting examples of camouflage does nature provide?

2. Which animals undergo changes in body coloration?

3. How does man utilize the concept of *camouflage*?

Camouflage helps animals survive in nature. It works in many different ways:

- Allows the animal to blend in with the background.
- Disrupts the body shape of the animal.
- Allows the animal to mimic a bad-tasting animal.
- Allows an animal to imitate a plant part.

Basic Steps to Follow

Materials:
- 9" x 12" (23 x 30 cm) white construction paper (1 per student plus one extra for the cover)
- 6" x 4 1/2" (15 x 11 cm) square of white construction paper (1 per student)
- writing paper cut to 6" x 4 1/2" (15 x 11 cm)
- scissors
- paste
- crayons or felt pens
- pencil
- a copy of the report form on page 127 (optional)
- paper fasteners

page 127

Directions:

1. Read about animals' ways of blending into their environment to escape predators. Brainstorm as many examples as possible. Make a list of them. Invite students to gather more information on these animals.

2. Each student selects a animal. Students read about this animal's camouflage tricks and any other ways nature has provided for this species. They will formulate a riddle about this animal to share with the class. They will write the riddle on the writing paper.

3. Students lay the riddle paper and the construction paper square on the larger white paper. Paste the riddle paper down.

4. Fold down the top edge of the white paper square. Paste it next to the riddle paper along this fold line. The picture of the animal will appear under this flap. Lightly trace around the square paper with a pencil. Now draw the animal inside the traced area.

5. Cut out a peek hole in the flap so that a part of the animal shows through. Now color the flap to resemble this animal's habitat. It needs to blend with the peek hole portion so that the camouflage effect is emphasized.

6. When all student riddles are complete, they may be asembled into a book. Add a cover and attach all the pieces on the left side with paper fasteners.

7. This lesson may be extended by using the report form on page 127. Students may do the report on their animal and then paste it on the back of the riddle form.

Gravity
A Gatefold Science Report

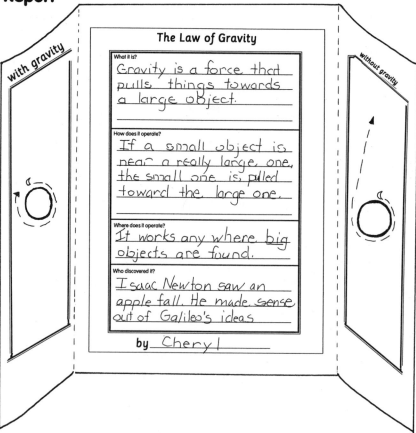

The Law of Gravity

What it is?
Gravity is a force that pulls things towards a large object.

How does it operate?
If a small object is near a really large one, the small one is pulled toward the large one.

Where does it operate?
It works any where big objects are found.

Who discovered it?
Isaac Newton saw an apple fall. He made sense out of Galileo's ideas

by Cheryl

with gravity

without gravity

Project:
Each student will create his/her own book on the topic of gravity. This project becomes a fine addition to a student's nonfiction writing portfolio.

Topics:

1. Develop a class discussion of the effects of gravity on our Earth: what it is and how it works.

2. Read about Issac Newton and how he discovered gravity. Is it true that he saw an apple fall from a tree branch and developed the theory of gravity?

3. Write a science fiction story about a world without gravity.

Gravity:
• the natural force that causes an attraction between any two bodies in space

• holds the planets in their orbits

• the natural force that causes objects in our atmosphere to be drawn toward the Earth

• causes objects to have weight on Earth

Basic Steps to Follow

Materials:

- 12" x 18" (30 x 46 cm) sheet of construction paper for each student
- writing and picture forms on pages 128 and 129
- stapler
- pencil
- felt pens or crayons

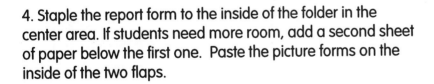

pages 128 and 129

Directions:

1. Use the information gathered during class discussions and reading to complete the writing form.

2. Illustrate the examples on the form labeled - *with and without.*

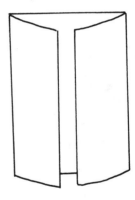

3. Fold both ends of the construction paper into the center. This is called a gatefold.

4. Staple the report form to the inside of the folder in the center area. If students need more room, add a second sheet of paper below the first one. Paste the picture forms on the inside of the two flaps.

5. Create a front cover that lists the title and the author. Decorate it with a picture that illustrates the topic.

Who Am I?

Animal Comparisons

A Class Riddle Book

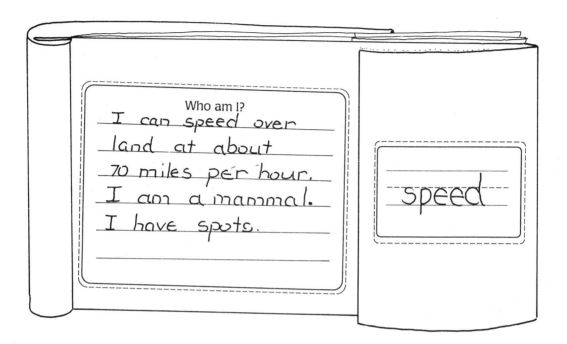

Who am I?
I can speed over land at about 70 miles per hour. I am a mammal. I have spots.

speed

Project:

Write riddles using animals as the topic. What animal is the fastest, the biggest, the noisiest? Encourage students to use the animal section in the nonfiction area of the library to gather their facts. Invite students to compare different animals and their most notable characteristics. Ask them to think about how those characteristics have allowed that species to survive.

Topics:

Which is the fastest?

Which is the biggest?

Which is the tallest?

Which is the noisiest?

Which animal has the longest nose?

Which animal is the best climber?

Which one has the best eyesight?

Which one has the best sense of smell?

Which one has the best sense of hearing?

Where to locate information:

- almanacs provide interesting statistics on animals
- animal encyclopedias
- nonfiction books

Basic Steps to Follow

Materials:

- 6" x 18" (15 x 46 cm) construction paper
- the writing form on page 130
- scissors
- felt pen or crayon
- pencil
- paste
- hole punch
- ribbon

page 130

Directions:

1. Students pick their animal and the quality of this animal that they will focus on. They research the topic and write a paragraph describing the animal <u>without</u> naming it. They may reveal where it lives, what it eats, and why its most unique characteristic has helped it survive. The paragraph is edited for corrections.

2. The final copy is written on the writing form. Then the picture of the animal is drawn in the space provided on the form. The *quality* that is being emphasized is written in the last box provided.

3. All three boxes are cut out.

4. The pieces are pasted to the construction paper as shown. The picture is pasted under the flap so that the reader can guess who the animal is before lifting the flap.

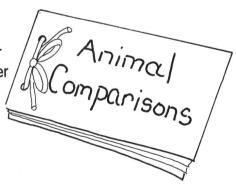

5. All student riddles are gather together. A cover is made from an extra sheet of construction paper folded in the same manner as the inside pages. The title is given on the left side of the paper and all student contributors are listed under the flap.

6. Punch holes in the left margin and tie it all together with a strip of ribbon.

Earthquake Shake-Up

A Book with Moving Parts

Project:

The moveable part of this student-authored book will motivate study and writing on the topic of earthquakes. Each student will have his/her own book to share with family and friends.

Topics:

1. General Information
   What is an earthquake?
   What causes it?
   Where do earthquakes usually occur?
   How are earthquakes measured?

2. Real-Life Experiences
   The day the Earth moved....
   I remember when....

Earthquake Information

When two pieces of land are separated by a fault line, the sides can move...

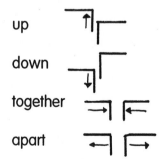

up

down

together

apart

When this happens, it sends vibrations in all directions that can cause damage to property.

Basic Steps to Follow

Materials:

- white construction paper cut to 8 1/2" x 4 1/2" (22 x 11 cm)
- 9" x 12" (23 x 30 cm) white construction paper for a background sheet
- 12" x 18" (30 x 46 cm) colored construction paper
- paper scraps to use in adding details
- writing paper
- scissors
- paste or glue
- ruler
- felt pens or crayons

Directions:

The Illustration

1. Each student will measure a 10" (25 cm) line in the center of the background sheet. Cut on that line.

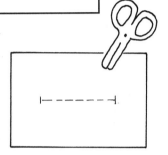

2. Fold the smaller sheet of construction paper in half. Slip one part of it in the slit that was cut in the background sheet. Move it back and forth to represent the earthquake movement at the fault line.

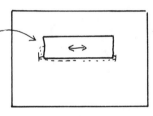

3. Use scrap paper and crayons or felt pen to add details to this landscape view. Objects may be pasted on or drawn directly on the background sheet. The objects placed on the moveable smaller piece of paper must be pasted to it and not to the background paper.

houses	trees
people	pets
cars	gardens

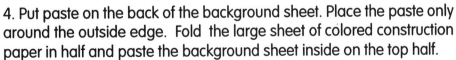

4. Put paste on the back of the background sheet. Place the paste only around the outside edge. Fold the large sheet of colored construction paper in half and paste the background sheet inside on the top half.

The Story

Write the story on standard horizontal writing paper. Paste the final copy on the bottom section below the illustration.

The Cover

The students fold the paper shut and decorate the cover of their book.

           How to Make Books with Children-Science & Math

Habitats
Mini-Pop-Ups

Project:

This project investigates the typical features of different habitats. It provides interesting opportunities for comparing and contrasting the habitats on our planet.

Topics:

1. What distinguishes one habitat from another?

2. What characteristics would a plant or animal have to have to survive in a special habitat?

3. The most important thing about a _____ is _____.

Extension Activities:

• Where are these habitats located? Why?

desert	delta
rainforest	slough
aquatic	subterranean
marine	urban
conifer forest	tundra
plains	

• Make a habitat map.

• Make a contour map in a sandbox showing landforms.

Basic Steps to Follow

Materials:

- 1 piece of 9" x 12" (23 x 30 cm) construction paper per student
- 3 pieces of 3" x 6" (7.5 x 15 cm) construction paper per student
- 3 pieces of 2" (5 cm) square pieces of white construction paper per student
- writing paper approximately 4" x 10" (10 x 26 cm)
- paste
- pencils
- crayon or felt pens
- ribbon
- hole punch

Directions:

1. Students research the habitat they have chosen. They write a paragraph describing the typical features and the plants and wildlife that live there. The final copy is copied on the writing paper.

2. Three mini-pop-ups are made to illustrate a typical plant, animal and weather pattern for this habitat. The pop-up is made with the 3" x 6" (7.5 x 15 cm) construction paper.

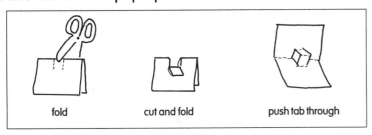

fold   cut and fold   push tab through

3. The pictures are drawn on the 2" (5 cm) square pieces. These pieces are then pasted to the front of the pop-up tab. Each pop-up is labeled on the front.

4. The students paste the paragraph and the pop-ups to the 9" x 12" (23 x 30 cm) construction paper.

5. All student reports are hole punched and bound together with a strip of ribbon. A cover is created listing the title and student contributors.

         How to Make Books with Children–Science & Math

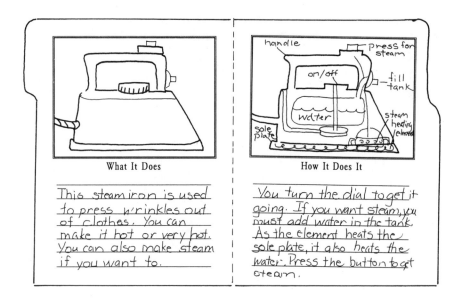

What It Does

This steam iron is used to press wrinkles out of clothes. You can make it hot or very hot. You can also make steam if you want to.

How It Does It

You turn the dial to get it going. If you want steam, you must add water in the tank. As the element heats the sole plate, it also heats the water. Press the button to get steam.

Project:

Each student researches "how something works." It could be a pencil sharpener or a steam iron. Let student curiosity be the motivator. All reports and diagrams are bound into file folders and filed alphabetically so that students can locate and share the information with classmates.

Topics:

1. A report on a mechanical or electrical appliance that a student is familiar with:
pencil sharpener, computer, calculator, telephone, mixer, toaster, steam iron, microwave, electric knife, food processor, television, stereo, etc.

2. A research project where a student must consult encyclopedias and other nonfiction resources to find out about inventions they want to know about, but have little experience with:

- rockets
- dump trucks
- subways
- submarines, factory machinery, etc.

Basic Steps to Follow

Materials:

- letter size file folders
- copies of the writing forms on pages 131 and 132
- stapler
- pencils
- crayons and felt pens

pages 131 and 132

Directions:

1. Brainstorm and list inventions that students are interested in learning more about. Assign each student a different invention.

2. Students may either do research in nonfiction books or do experiments on an actual appliance to investigate how it works.

3. Each report will have two diagrams. One will show what the invention looks like and the other will be a cross section showing the working parts and how they interact. A written explanation accompanies the diagrams.

4. After rough drafts are approved, the final report is completed. The forms are stapled to the inside of a file folder.

5. The outside of the file folder is entitled *Technology Encyclopedia* and is labeled with the beginning sound and title of the invention. All the folders should be placed alphabetically in a box on a shelf so that students can use them as a resource.

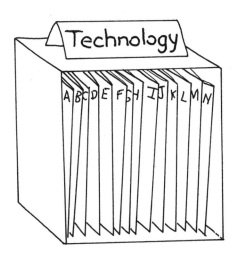

Journey Through the Solar System

An Individual File Folder Book

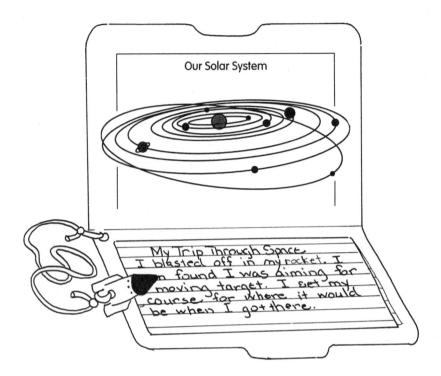

Our Solar System

My Trip Through Space.
I blasted off in my rocket. I
soon found I was aiming for
a moving target. I set my
course for where it would
be when I got there.

Project:

Students use the facts they have learned about the solar system to construct a fictional story based on scientific facts.

Topics:

1. *My Trip to _____.* Students may choose to write about a trip to any planet in our solar system. It will require them to know basic information about distances between planets, atmospheres on other planets, etc.

2. Perhaps students will write on a topic like *Lost in Space.* They would have to come up with survival solutions to this dilemma and a clever plan about how to get back to planet Earth.

3. What would an aspiring astronaut need to pack for a trip like this? What sort of basic supplies are required and for how long?

How far away are the planets from the sun?

Planet	Distance (miles)	Distance (km)
Mercury -	36,000,000 miles	58,000,000 km
Venus -	67,000,000 miles	108,000,000 km
Earth -	93,000,000 mile	150,000,000 km
Mars -	143,000,000 miles	230,000,000 km
Jupiter -	483,000,000 miles	778,000,000 km
Saturn -	890,000,000 miles	1,433,000,000 km
Uranus -	1,779,000,000 miles	2,863,000,000 km
Neptune-	2,807,000,000 miles	4,518,000,000 km
Pluto -	3,666,000,000 miles	5,900,000,000 km

Basic Steps to Follow

Materials:

- letter size file folder for each student
- outer space form on page 133
- writing paper
- 3" x 5" (7 x 13 cm) file cards cut in half
- yarn or string
- pencil
- crayon or felt pens
- hole punch
- paste

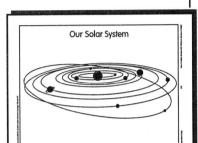

Our Solar System

page 133

Directions:

1. Students plan their journey and write a rough draft. The story is shared with a student editor and corrections to spelling, grammar, and content are made. The final draft is completed. Students may use as many sheets of paper as needed to complete the story.

2. The diagram of the solar system is colored.

3. The story and the diagram are pasted inside the file folder.

4. A spaceship or rocket is designed and colored in on 1/2 of the file card. It is cut out and a hole is punched in one corner.

5. A hole is punched in the folder. A strip of yarn or string is tied through the hole. The other end of the yarn is attached to the rocket or spaceship.

6. The rocket may then be used to move about the diagram of the solar system as the journey unfolds as a part of the story.

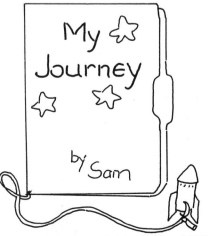

My ☆ Journey ☆ ☆ by Sam

7. Each student should design a cover for his/her story on the front of the file folder.

A Book about Changes and Their Causes
Before and After
A Flap Book

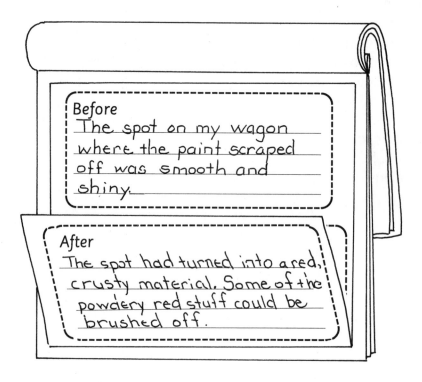

Before
The spot on my wagon where the paint scraped off was smooth and shiny.

After
The spot had turned into a red, crusty material. Some of the powdery red stuff could be brushed off.

Project:

Encourage students to think about how things change in our world. Sometimes change is automatic because of the natural course of events, but sometimes the change is <u>caused</u> to happen.

Topics:

Physical Changes
- melting
- expanding
- dissolving
- grinding

Biological Changes
- aging
- hatching
- metamorphosis
- flowering

Chemical Changes
- burning
- combining atoms
- rusting
- separating atoms

Basic Steps to Follow

Materials:
- the writing form on page 134
- 9" x 12" (23 x 30 cm) construction paper
- paste
- pencil
- crayons or felt pens
- paper fasteners

page 134

Directions:

1. Brainstorm *Before and After* circumstances. Suggest a few that might stretch students' knowledge. After noting a typical change in nature, they must then locate information as to the scientific reason for the change.

leaf...fossil	acid on metal....hole
water....ice	coffee bean......brewed coffee
batter....bread	blossom....fruit
flat balloon....floating balloon	tadpole .....frog
river.....erosion on bank	egg....chicken
dirty clothes ....clean clothes	caterpillar....butterfly
log....ashes	iron...rust

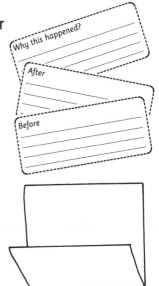

2. Complete the writing form sections.

3. Fold up a flap on the bottom of the construction paper sheet. Cut apart the writing form sections and paste them as shown.

4. Collect all student contributions. Add a construction paper cover. Attach everything together across the top with paper fasteners. Place this volume in the classroom library.

How Did That Happen?

A Pull-Tab Book

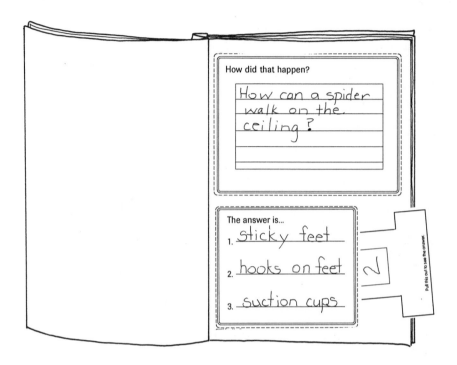

Project:

Students pose a riddle that will make us think. They begin with a scientific theory and then list several explanations of this theory. The reader of the riddle must pick the explanation that is the correct one. The answer is hidden inside the pull-out tab.

Topics:

This format is adjustable to many topics in your science curriculum. How often we hear the words "How does that happen?" This project provides an opportunity to seek out the answers to some of these questions.

    1. How can an airplane fly?

    2. How can a spider walk on the ceiling?

    3. How can a water drop make a rainbow?

    4. How can food turn into your body?

    5. How can a huge ship float?

                How to Make Books with Children-Science & Math

Basic Steps to Follow

Materials:

- 9" x 12" (23 x 46 cm) construction paper
- reproducible writing forms on pages 135 and 136
- paste
- pencil
- scissors
- paper fasteners

pages 135 and 136

Directions:

1. Students establish the question they want to ask and fill out the form
How does _____?

2. Then the possible answers have to be listed. This is the creative part of the project. Each possible answer should contain a shred of truth so that readers of this riddle will have a more difficult time picking the correct answer.

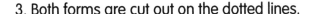

3. Both forms are cut out on the dotted lines.

4. The question and the answer forms are pasted in place on the construction paper sheet. Paste is only applied around the top, left side, and bottom of the answer form.

5. The real answer is written on the tab portion of the form. The answer tab form is cut out and slipped into the opening on the right side of the answer form.

6. Collect all class riddle sheets, add a cover and bind them together with paper fasteners.

The Night Sky
A Silhouette Book

The Night Sky
When I look out at night,
I see the moon and the stars.
If I look a long time, I
see things change.

When I look out at night
I also see night creatures
searching for food. Last night
I saw a bat dive down to
catch a mouse.
by JoEllen

Project:

Student may use this project to tell about actual sightings in the night sky or as a report on information gathered from books in the library.

Topics:

1. Write about the typical characteristics of objects that might be seen in the night sky:

stars	meteors
moon	constellations
planets	satellites
asteroids	airplanes
comets	

2. Write about wildlife often sighted in the night sky: bats, owls, fireflies, etc.

3. Plan a trip to a place seen in the night sky.

4. Describe what the planet Earth must look like from out there.

Basic Steps to Follow

Materials:
- 12" x 18" (30 x 46 cm) dark blue construction paper
- 4 1/2" x 12" (25 x 30 cm) black construction paper
- scraps of white, yellow and black construction paper
- horizontally orientated writing paper
- scissors
- paste
- stapler
- yellow and white tempera paint (optional)
- cut-up sponges and pencil erasers (optional)

Directions:

1. Decide on a topic and research the information. Develop a rough draft of the report and have it edited. Copy it in final form on the writing paper.

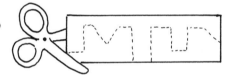

2. Paste the writing paper to the lower portion of the dark blue construction paper.

3. The illustration begins with a silhouette skyline image of trees or buildings cut from the black construction paper. Paste this strip above the story.

4. What appears in the night sky? Cut out construction paper shapes or use sponge and eraser prints with tempera paint or crayon pictures to illustrate the images that are being discussed in the report.

5. Involve a student in creating an interesting cover for this book. Use some of the techniques used in the illustrations: cut and paste, printing, or coloring.

Simple Machines
How We Got the Job Done
A Flap Book

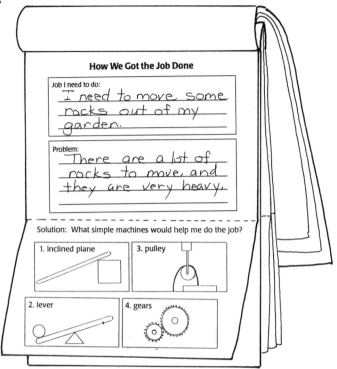

How We Got the Job Done

Job I need to do:
I need to move some rocks out of my garden.

Problem:
There are a lot of rocks to move, and they are very heavy.

Solution: What simple machines would help me do the job?

1. inclined plane

3. pulley

2. lever

4. gears

Project:

Each student creates his/her own book of simple machines with a description of how they work for us. Invite students at all levels to investigate how these simple machines comprise many of the more complicated inventions that we use everyday.

Topics:

We are building a rock wall in the garden. How will we move all of this rock from the front of the house to the back?

We are making a tree house. How will we get all of the wood and equipment up there?

We have to move these heavy boxes into the truck. We can't lift them that high. What can we do?

Simple Machines:

• Inclined Plane

•Gears

• Lever

• Pulley

A simple machine is a device that allows you to do a job with less force. However, you pay for it by having to work longer or make more trips. It's worth it if the job would otherwise be too hard or impossible to do.

Basic Steps to Follow

Materials:

- the writing form on page 137
- sheet of white copy paper
- crayons or felt pens
- paste
- 2 pieces of tagboard for covers
- scissors
- stapler
- duct tape

page 137

Directions:

1. Students propose a job that needs to be done. Then they state the *Problem* they would face doing this job without benefit of simple machines.

2. Now the student plans how the use of simple machines can make this job easier. He/She illustrates on the white construction paper the machines they feel are best suited to this task.

3. The writing form is folded up on the dotted line and pasted to the blank copy paper.

4. All student pages are bound together across the top and titled *How We Got the Job Done.* Create a hinged cover for the book following the directions on page 3. Staple the cover and pages together. Cover the binding with duct tape.

5. As students read the book, they will try to guess, before looking under the flap, how the job was accomplished and which simple machines were used. Can they think of others that would have been more useful?

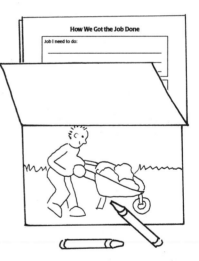

Questions About My Body
A Question and Answer Book

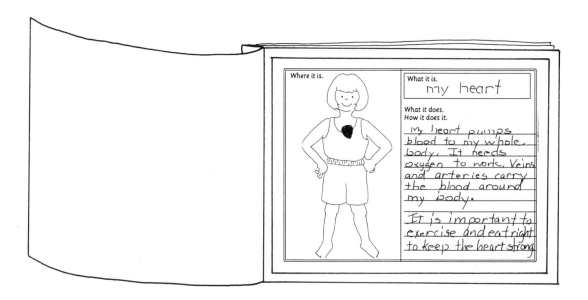

Project:

How does our heart serve us? Is the pancreas critical to our survival? Use this opportunity to become more familiar with how our bodies function.

Topics:

Do research on organs of the body:

brain
heart
lungs
liver
kidneys
stomach
intestines
bones
muscles
blood
skin
pancreas

Extension Activities:

Trace these phenomena to their cause.

What causes a sneeze?

What causes a cough?

What causes a yawn?

What is a hiccup?

What is a burp?

What causes tears?

Why do we perspire?

Basic Steps to Follow

Materials:

- a copy of the writing form on page 138
- 9" x 12" (23 x 30 cm) sheets of construction paper
- pencil
- crayon or felt pen
- paste
- hole punch
- shoelace

page 138

Directions:

1. Students each select a topic. They use resources at the library and gather answers to questions on the topic.

2. Students write a rough draft, have it checked by a student editor, then copy the final draft on the writing form.

3. Diagram the body on the writing form to illustrate the topic being discussed.

4. Paste the writing form to the construction paper.

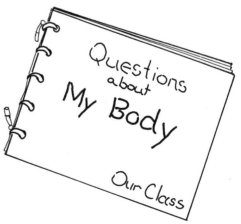

5. Collect the class questions and answers and bind them together. Punch five holes in the left margin.
Wind the shoelace (as shown) through the holes.

Animal Classifications

A Brown Paper Bag Book

Project:

How is the animal kingdom divided? What characteristics do each of the groups share? Can animals be classified in other ways?

Topics:

Vertebrates
Invertebrates

Mammals
Reptiles
Insects
Amphibians
Birds

Carnivores
Vegetarians

Domesticated
Wild

Flying
Swimming
Crawling

Huge
Tiny

Basic Steps to Follow

Materials:

- one large brown paper bag for each page in the book
- report form on page 139
- hole punch
- yarn
- crayons or felt pens
- writing paper
- white construction paper

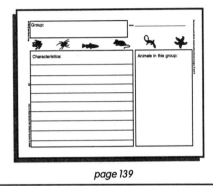

page 139

Directions:

The Book

1. Create the brown paper bag book:

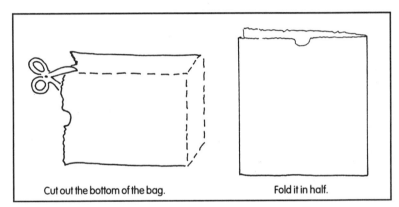

Cut out the bottom of the bag.   Fold it in half.

2. Bind the book. Collect the pages from students. Punch three holes in the left margin. Wind the yarn through the holes and design a cover for the book.

The Report Pages

1. Brainstorm the classifications the students are going to explore. Assign each student or cooperative group a topic to research. Give them the report form to guide them. They are to list the major characteristics of their particular group and gather names and pictures of the animals that belong in the group.

2. Give each group one brown paper bag page. Paste the report form and the illustrations on this page. The illustrations may be done by the students or they may be collected from magazines.

What Causes Seasons?

A Newspaper Book

Project:

Each student will write his/her own book on seasonal changes on our planet. Why do they happen? Why is it different in various parts of the world?

Topics:

Discuss the pathway of the Earth around the sun. How does that create seasonal changes?

What effect does the axis of the Earth have on this question?

Which hemisphere of the Earth do we live in? Does that affect our climate?

Why?
The Earth travels once around the sun every 365 days, 5 hours, 48 minutes and 46 seconds. While Earth is making this orbit, it is also spinning on its axis. The axis is tilted sideways in relation to the sun.
So for part of the year the northern hemisphere faces away from the sun and the southern hemisphere leans toward the sun. These positions change as the Earth orbits. This change in position creates the fluctuations in temperatures that we call seasons.

How to Make Books with Children-Science & Math

Basic Steps to Follow

Materials:

- 3 newspaper sheets per student
- 3" x 12" (7.5 x 30 cm) strip of construction paper for the binding
- a copy of the writing form and diagram page for each student on pages 140 and 141
- crayons or felt pens
- scissors
- stapler
- paste

pages 140 and 141

Directions:

The Newspaper Book

1. Fold the newspaper sheet twice.

2. Staple three sheets together in the left margin.
Fold the construction paper strip in half.
Wrap it around the spine and paste in place.

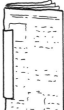

The Story

1. The author has five pages of space to develop.
There is the front cover and then one page per season.

2. Provide students with a writing form sheet and Earth-sun diagram for each season. Students may choose to write a scientific explanation of each season, or they may want to weave scientific data into a fictional story with characters and a simple plot.

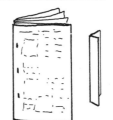

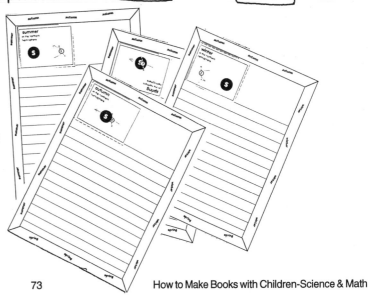

Volcanoes
A Three-Fold Book

Project:

Investigate how and why volcanoes erupt. Reinforce what the class learns by inviting each student to create his/her own book on volcanoes that illustrates how volcanoes act.

Topics:

Where are volcanoes found?

What is an eruption?

Are all volcanoes and eruptions the same?

How do volcanic rocks differ?

General Information...

1. Our Earth is composed of layers of rock. The outer layer is called the *crust*. Below this crust there are pockets of melted rock called *magma*.
2. A *volcano* is created when magma pushes up through cracks in the Earth's surface.
3. When the magma erupts from the volcano it is called *lava*.
4. When the lava cools and hardens, it forms a layer of *igneous rock*.
5. Volcanoes usually happen along cracks in the Earth's crust called *plates*. Often there are eruptions under the ocean and the volcanic eruption creates an island.

Basic Steps to Follow

Materials:

- 9" x 12" (23 x 30 cm) sheet of brown construction paper
- a copy of the diagram and writing form on pages 142 and 143
- 5" (13 cm) square piece of white construction paper
- black and red tempera paint
- sponge pieces
- crayon or felt pens
- paste

pages 142 and 143

Directions:

1. Color and cut out the volcano diagram. Discuss and label the parts shown in this cross section.

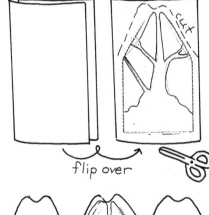

2. Paste the diagram in the center of the brown paper. Fold the sides around it. Fold the flaps to the back. Cut along the top of the volcano through all the layers.

3. Do research on volcanoes and write about how and why they erupt. Cut out the two writing boxes. Open the flaps on the brown construction paper. Paste the two writing sections on the inside flaps on each side of the diagram.

4. Close the right-hand flap. Use sponges and tempera paint to create the impression of hot lava and hardened igneous rock at the top of the volcano. Cut out the puff of smoke and paste it to this layer.

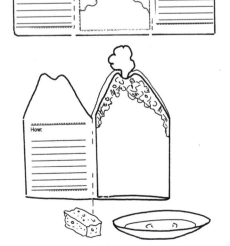

5. Close the left-hand flap and look at the front cover. Use paper scraps or felt pens to design the outside of the volcano.

My Science Journal

Daily Record Keeping

Project:

Use this form to create student science journals to record daily vocabulary and observations that reinforce what they have learned in science.

Topic:

1. Today I learned.....

2. Vocabulary I Want to Remember

3. Science Books with Interesting Facts

4. Topics I Want to Read More About

My Very Own Journal...

Collect the journal pages from each student and bind them together into book form. Provide tagboard cut to the same size as the journal forms to use as front and back covers.

Show students how to do the hinged binding (See page 3). They can create sturdy, attractive journals to use throughout the year.

---

name:

date:

topic:

My Science Journal
Take a closer look at our world.

How to Make Books with Children-Science & Math

How to Make Books with Children-Science & Math

Student-Authored

MATH

BOOKS

Counting Sheep

A Do and Learn Book

Counting Sheep

by Jose.
I saw 6 sheep grazing on the hill. Then another two sheep ran out from behind a big bush. Those sheep and 2 of the six ran away. How many were left?

Project:
Students are challenged to create story problems on the topic of sheep. The problems they write are bound together in this book. Sheep counters are provided so that students can work through the problems as they read them. The answers will available on the back of each page.

Topics:

1. Counting the sheep on the hill:
   - 1-10
   - Count by 2

> *Mother sent me out to get the sheep. I counted them as they went through the gate. I had more than 12 but less than 14. How many did I have?*

2. Story problems involving addition, subtraction, multiplication or division

> *Five sheep were grazing on the hill. Two sheep slipped under the fence and ran down the road.*
> *How many sheep were left on the hill?*

3. Practice with number words and ordinals.

Basic Steps to Follow

Materials:
- green tagboard for the cover:
  11" x 12" (28 x 30.5 cm) and 6 1/2" x 12" (16 x 30.5 cm)
- a sheet of 6" x 11" (15 x 28 cm) writing paper for each student
- construction paper scraps
- an envelope
- several copies of the reproducible sheep patterns on page 144
- felt pens
- 2 paper fasteners
- pencils
- scissors
- glue
- hole punch

page 144

Directions:

The Cover

1. Cut the front and back cover from the green tagboard. Add the fence and other details with paper scraps and felt pens.

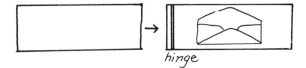

hinge

2. Hinge the front cover. See the directions on page 3.

3. Adhere the envelope to the front cover. Write the title on the envelope.

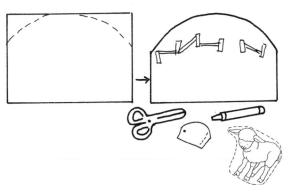

4. Cut out the sheep and put them in the envelope. Make as many as are needed to solve the story problems.

The Pages

1. Each student writes a story problem about sheep.

2. They may use a folded piece of construction paper scrap to hide the answer to the problem. Paste the answer to the back of each sheet.

The Book

1. Collect all the pages. Bind them inside the cover using paper fasteners.

2. Make the book available for students to share. They can take out the sheep and place them on the green construction paper hill to help them answer each question. The answer should be on the back of the sheet.

Skip-Counting Fun

A Drop-Down Pleated Book

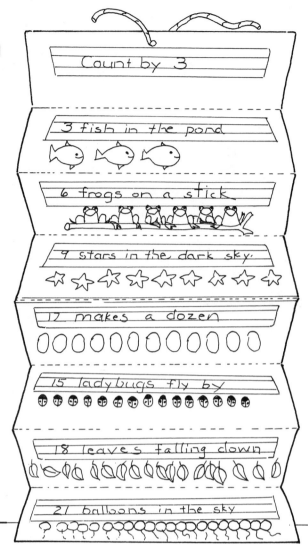

Count by 3

3 fish in the pond

6 frogs on a stick

9 stars in the dark sky.

12 makes a dozen

15 ladybugs fly by

18 leaves falling down

21 balloons in the sky

Project:

Give students the opportunity to practice skip-counting and writing skills in the same project. This type of project is good to use with a cooperative group. Each student can easily make a contribution and not feel overwhelmed by the project.

Topics:

1. Learn the jingle:

    2, 4, 6, 8
    Who do we appreciate?

2. Practice skip counting with any pattern:

    2, 4, 6, 8, 10, 12, 14, 16, 18, etc.
    3, 6, 9, 12, 15, 18, 21, etc.
    5, 10, 15, 20, 25, 30, 35, etc.
    10, 20, 30, 40, 50, 60, etc.

The illustrations may be of different objects (somehow related) or all the same object. You may require a rhyming pattern or leave the writing style up to the student.

Basic Steps to Follow

Materials:

- 2 sheets of 12" x 18" (30 x 46 cm) colored construction paper
- tape
- hole punch
- ribbon
- 8 pieces of 2" x 10" (5 x 25 cm) writing paper
- pencil
- crayons or felt pens
- paste

Directions:

1. Fold the construction paper sheets into quarters.

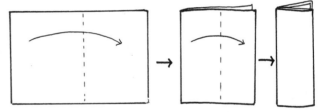

2. Tape the two pieces of construction paper end-to-end. Refold the folds so they are accordion folded.

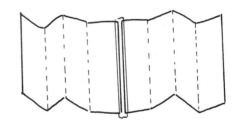

3. Glue a piece of writing paper in each segment.

4. Draw and color as many items as necessary to illustrate that section.

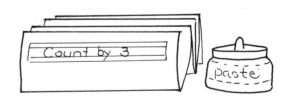

5. Punch a hole at the top of the first section. Slip the ribbon through it. It may either be used to hold the accordion-pleated book closed or it may be used to hang it up for display.

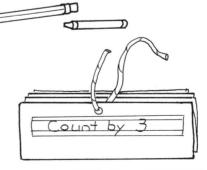

     How to Make Books with Children–Science & Math

Monkey Chain Magic

A Do and Learn Book

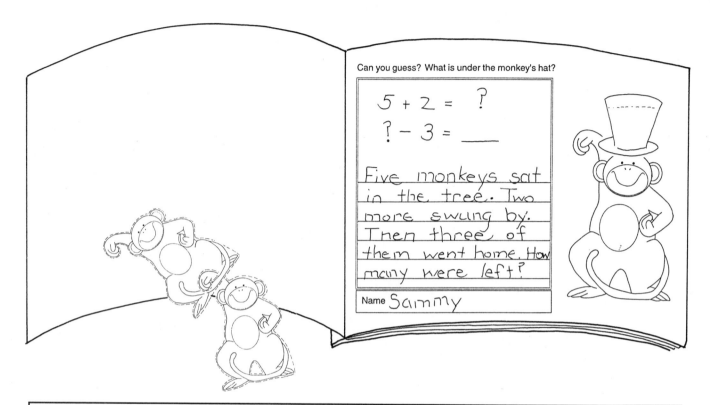

Can you guess? What is under the monkey's hat?

$5 + 2 = ?$

$? - 3 = \_\_\_$

Five monkeys sat in the tree. Two more swung by. Then three of them went home. How many were left?

Name Sammy

Project:

Students will set up the problems and use the monkeys that hook together to check their answers. This book will be shared again and again because they will love to participate in the solutions.

Topics:

1. Basic Addition and Subtraction Practice

2. Multi-stepped Story Problems

3. Ordinal Number Practice

Basic Steps to Follow

Materials:

- *Can You Guess* worksheet on page 146 for each student
- 9" x 12" (23 x 30 cm) construction paper for the back cover
- 12" x 13" (30 x 33 cm) construction paper for the front cover
- several sheets of the reproducible monkey and hat patterns on page 145
- stapler
- crayons
- paste
- scissors
- paper fasteners
- hole punch

pages 145 and 146

Directions:

The Front Cover
1. Fold up 4" (10 cm) on the bottom of the 13" (33 cm) sheet to create a pocket.
2. Write the title *Monkey Chain Magic.*
3. Cut out the monkey patterns and slip them into the pocket.

The Pages
1. Students make up their own equations.
2. They color the monkey and paste one of the hat patterns on monkey's head.
3. They write the answer to the problem in the area under the monkey's hat.

The Book
1. Place student pages inside the covers.
2. Punch holes and insert paper fasteners in the left margin.
3. Put the monkeys in the pocket.

How to Use:
The students read the problems. They hook the monkeys together to make a chain to represent the numbers in that equation. They check under the monkey's hat to see if they are right. This book is a wonderful learning center all by itself.

Math Riddles

A Flap Book

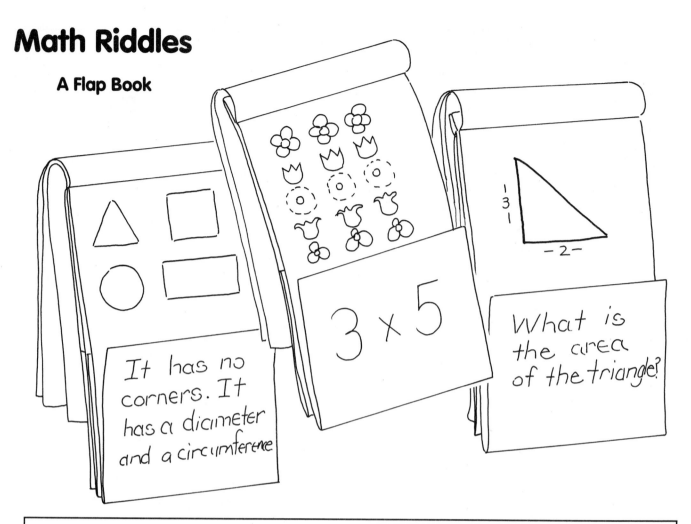

Project:

This easy-to-make book reinforces several math concepts children need to know. The level of the material is adaptable. What do your students need to practice?

Topics:

1. Number Words - one, two, three, four, five, six, seven, eight, nine, ten, etc.
2. Sets - 0-10 or 2, 4, 6, 8, etc.
3. Addition Equations - 1+1, 2+1, 3+1, etc.
4. Multiplication Equations - 3 x 1, 4 x 1, 5 x 1, etc.
5. Ordinal Numbers - first, second, third, fourth, fifth, sixth, etc.
6. Shapes - square, oval, circle, hexagon, triangle, rectangle, etc.
7. Algebraic Equations
8. Solid Geometry

Basic Steps to Follow

Materials:

- 6" x 18" (15 x 46 cm) white construction paper for the inside pages
- 12" x 6" (30 x 15 cm) colored construction paper for the cover
- scratch paper for a rough plan sheet
- felt pens or crayons
- pencil
- ruler
- stapler
- scissors

Directions:

Beginning
Make a list of the numbers, number words or concepts that you want the students to practice. Assign each student one of these. They plan their work on scratch paper.

Inside Pages
1. Fold over 6" (15 cm) on one side of the long white paper.

2. Set the paper up in the following format: Each student must follow the general format. Hidden under the flap is information that expands the concept.

The Cover
1. Collect papers.

2. Design a cover that lists the title and the authors.

3. Assemble the pages and the cover. Staple them together across the top.

4. Share the book with other students. Can they guess what is hidden under the flap?

Subtraction Practice

How Many Were Left?

A Koala Shape Book

Handwritten note in koala's pouch: "...oala ate 24 ...calyptus leaves. ...hen he picked ...more. He gave ...ay 10. How Many Were Left?"

Cover: How Many Were Left? by Lee

Project:

Students will each create their own book practicing subtraction skills. The books may be a collection of word problems or they may be a fictional story where subtraction is involved in the storyline. The koala jar may hold anything: cookies, ants, fireflies, pencils, water, etc.

Topics:

1. Each student writes a series of word problems to share with other students. The problems will involve a subraction equation each time. The illustration area for each problem will show the solution pictorially. Students will decorate their covers and staple all the pages together.

2. It becomes a more involved process when students have to plan a story where subtraction is a theme that continues to happen. The student would begin by developing characters and a setting. Then they would plan a plot. This plot may take several pages to work to a conclusion. Each page of the story should involve some item in the story being diminished.

Koala had six eucalyptus leaves in his lunch. But when it was time to eat, there were only three in the pouch. How many were missing?

When Koala went for a walk, she counted the trees so she wouldn't get lost. She counted 9 trees in a row. But on her way home she went too far. She counted 12 trees. How far back did she have to go?

Basic Steps to Follow

Materials:

- a cover form on page 147
- the writing form on page 148
- 9" x 12" (23 x 30 cm) construction paper

- crayons or felt pens
- pencils
- stapler
- scissors
- paste

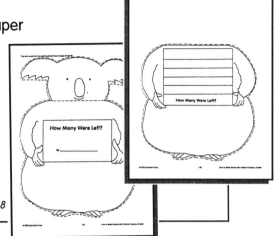

pages 147 and 148

Directions:

1. What is inside this koala jar? Each student formulates his/her story plan or word problems on the writing form. They develop as many of these pages as they want and then cut them on the dotted line.

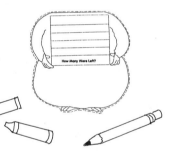

2. Students color the koala cover form and cut it out. Then they cut off the koala's head on the dotted line.

3. Students paste the koala's head and the writing sheet to the construction paper. The other writing sheets and koala's body are stapled on top along the left side.

4. Student pages are put together. Add a construction paper cover and staple along the left margin.

89

Can You Make It?
Tangram Fun
An Activity Book

This is Stan. He is now extinct. He lived in a jungle. He ate plants. He loved red berries. He ate so many he turned all red. Now he eats blueberries!

by Mary

Tangram Fun

Project:

Each student contributes one page to this book with a design created from tangram patterns. The reader is provided with a set of tangrams and tries to recreate the design on each page.

Topics:

Each student has a double task. They will create the tangram pattern and a description of the design. The description may be one paragraph about the design or it may be a story created with the tangram figure as the main character.

Basic Steps to Follow

Materials:

- the tangram patterns on page 149
- the writing form on page 150
- 12" x 18" (30 x 46 cm) construction paper
- 9" x 12" (23 x 30 cm) construction paper
- scissors
- felt pens or crayons
- stapler

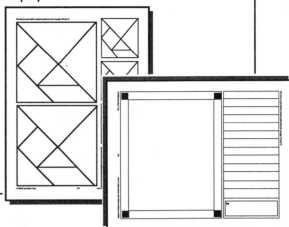

pages 149 and 150

Directions:

Individual Pages

1. Students plan their tangram shape. They lightly trace around the tangram pattern pieces to create the design. They color in the entire area with a solid color (the separate tangram pieces should not be visible).

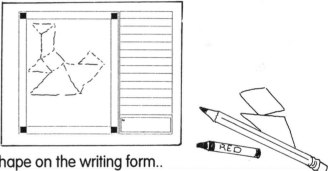

2. Students write a story or explanation of the shape on the writing form..

3. All student pages are collected together.

The Binding

1. Fold up the bottom 4" (10 cm) of the large construction paper. Staple this flap closed on the two sides.
Place a set of tangrams for students to play with in this flap.

2. Design a cover for the book on the smaller sheet of construction paper. Print the title and the name of the authors. Staple this cover and the students' papers above the flap that holds the tanpagegrams.

91   How to Make Books with Children-Science & Math

Measuring Worm
An Activity File Folder Book

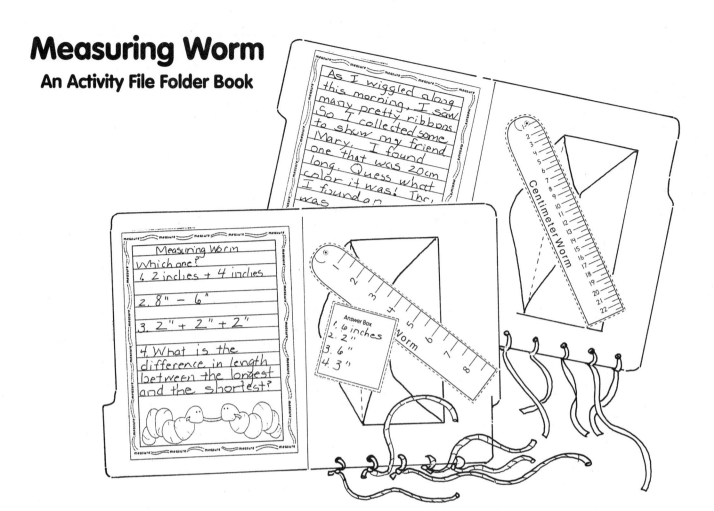

Project:

Students practice measurement skills and create an activity book for other classmates to share. The book contains forms or stories about a little worm who loves to measure. Attached to the book are yarn strips that exactly match the lengths being discussed in the stories. Readers have to find which strip of colored yarn goes with or answers each story problem.

Topics:

1. Fill in the blank.
Provide each student with the form on page 152. Let students write story problems and then cut yarn strips to match the answers.

2. Write a story.
Students with more writing experience may use the same form to construct a story about this worm who loved to measure everything he saw. This could take the form of a riddle where the reader has to guess what is being measured.

Basic Steps to Follow

Materials:

- worm form on page 151
- writing form on page 152
- yarn or ribbon in many different colors
- #10 letter envelope
- file folder
- scissors
- hole punch
- pencil
- crayons or felt pens
- tape
- stapler
- glue
- a small piece of tagboard   *pages 151 and 152*

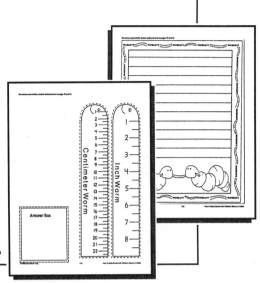

Directions:

1. Let students plan their story or word problems.

2. Provide yarn in many colors for them to cut off the length they use in their story. Have them cut the yarn longer than they need. They will cut it to exact measurements later.

3. Punch holes along the bottom of the file folder. The yarn strips are tied on. Now they are cut to match the measurements in the story problems.

4. Tape the envelope to the file folder. Make a copy of the measuring worm and glue it to tagboard. Place the worm in the envelope.

5. Staple the writing form to the left side of the folder.

6. Fill out the answer card and slip it in the envelope with the worm.

7. Design a front cover for the book. Give the title and the authors' names.

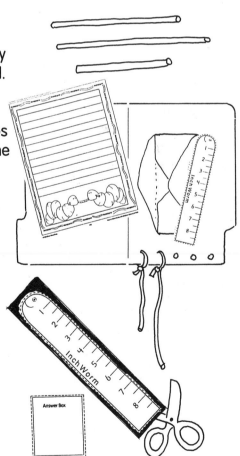

Fraction Practice
Cut It Up
A Shape Book

Project:

Use this easily adaptable project to fit many themes: pizza, pies, cakes, cookies. Students become involved in creating stories where fractional parts of the whole turn up missing. How much is gone? How much is left? How much did each get? etc.

Topics:

1. Story Problems
   - *I made a chocolate pie. I cut the pie to feed four people.*
     How much did each person get?
   - *My mother made pizza for dinner.*
     We each want two pieces.
     There are four of us at home.
     How many pieces did she cut?

2. Write a Story
   The Day I Made a Surprise Cake
   The Magic Pizza
   Who Ate the Pie?
   The 1/2 Cookie Thief

Basic Steps to Follow

Materials:

- writing forms on page 153 (2 per student)
- 6" x 18" (15 x 46 cm) construction paper
- construction paper scraps in several colors
- scissors
- paste
- pencil
- crayons or felt pens

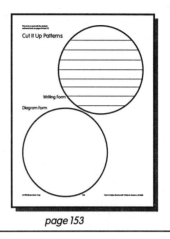

page 153

Directions:

1. Fold the construction paper strip into thirds.

2. Round the corners to create the cover of the book. It may turn out to be a cookie, a pie, a pizza or a cake.

3. Use the writing form and diagram form to create the story problems. After the writing forms and illustrations are complete, paste them to the construction paper book cover.

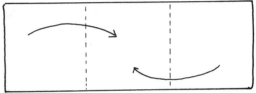

| *a. cover* | *b. story problem and illustration (open left section)* | *c. continuation of story problem (open right section)* | *d. the answers (on the back)* |

Mix and Measure
Invent a Recipe
A Class Book of Recipes

My Recipe

Name: Paul

Name of Recipe: chocolate mousse

Ingredients:

milk   chocolate

sugar   salt

Steps to follow:
1. Heat the milk. It will boil. Stop it then.
2. Put the chocolate into melt in the milk.
3. Stir in sugar and salt.
4. Let it cool and get thick. Eat with cookies.

Project:

Students create fictional recipes using measuring cups and spoons as methods of measurement. The resulting recipe book may then be used by the class in a center to experiment with real measuring cups and spoons.

Topics:

1. Pick a favorite character from literature. Plan a recipe that would fit that character's taste exactly.

> What would Peter Rabbit want for tea?
> Create a new cookie for that little mouse.
> What is it that Frances would like for a snack?
> Would Lyle want raisins in his oatmeal?

Each recipe would list the number of cups or liters or spoons for each ingredient.

2. Younger children could pick one ingredient to add to a class recipe. Their sentence would state the ingredient, the amount, and why it is included.

3. Create a story about a magic ingredient that a student might add to any recipe. What is it? How much is necessary? What is the effect?

Basic Steps to Follow

Materials:

- the writing form on page 154
- the cup/spoon form on page 155
- 9" x 12" (23 x 46 cm) construction paper
- pencils
- crayons or felt pens
- stapler
- paste
- scissors

pages 154 and 155

Directions:

1. Students plan the recipe. They will use the measuring cups and spoons patterns to show how much of an ingredient is needed in the recipe.

2. Then students are to tell step-by-step what needs to be done to make the recipe.

3. The class papers are collected together. A cover is created from construction paper. Make a border with the measuring cups and spoons patterns and have each student sign one.

Extension:

Place this recipe book in a center with a set of measuring cups and tubs of uncooked rice or beans and a mixing bowl. Let students practice measuring as they concoct these entertaining recipes.

Build a Thousand

A Brown Paper Bag Book

Project:

Let children participate in building sets of 100. Each page of this book will picture 100 "things." Groups of children work together to create these pages and then they combine their pages with the other groups to create even bigger numbers.

Topics:

Build a thousand of something. Each cooperative group is responsible for creating 10 sets of ten. The topics may be assigned or they may evolve from a theme: insects, plants, candy, flags, foods, or basic shapes. The real emphasis here is for students to actually experience **100 of something**. Then when ten hundreds are placed together, a **thousand of something** will be the result.

Basic Steps to Follow

Materials:

- large brown shopping bags
- the forms on pages 156-158
- crayons or felt pens
- scissors
- pencils
- paste
- 3 paper fasteners

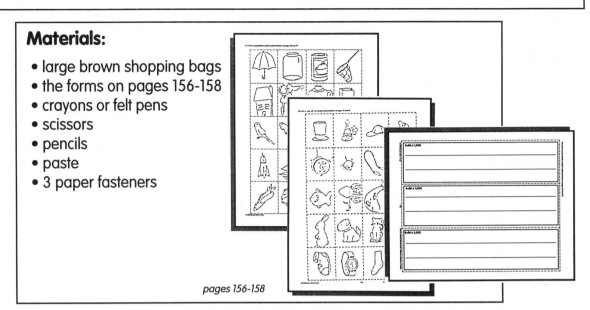

pages 156-158

Directions:

1. Brainstorm the classifications the students are going to create. Students may use the form provided to create their sets or they may cut sets out of construction paper.

2. Create the brown paper bag book:

3. The group draws, colors and cuts out their sets. They will paste them on the brown bag. When they are finished they should have 10 rows of items with ten in each row. All the items on the page may be the same or each row may feature a different theme.

4. They are to write one sentence summarizing what is on this page on the writing form provided.
    100 spiders
    100 squares
    100 ladybugs, etc.

5. When 10 pages are done, they are put together to make a book of a thousand. Students may choose to make several copies of these books until they have created a million!

6. A cover is designed for the book and it is bound together with three paper fasteners.

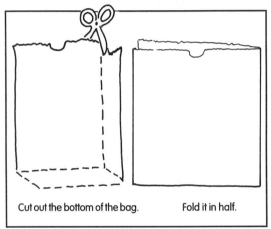

Cut out the bottom of the bag.   Fold it in half.

The Big and Little

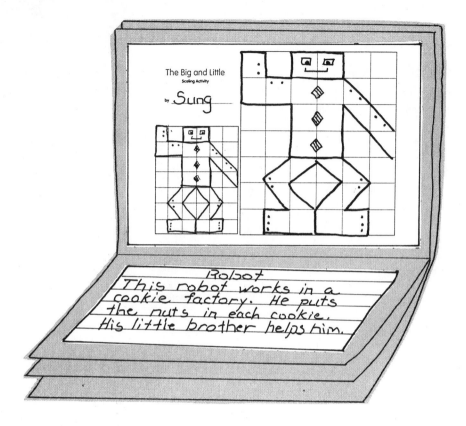

Project:

This project asks students to scale a small illustration into a larger form. It requires close attention to detail and a careful attention to the graph to represent the second picture accurately. Angular objects will be easier to create than curved objects.

Topics:

1. Explain how the image grew larger.

2. Explain how the image was made smaller.

3. Make up a story about the characters or scene shown in the picture.

Who uses scaling?

• Architects make scale models of buildings to help in planning.

• Astronomers make scale models to make huge sizes and distances easier to understand.

• Artists and sculpters make scale models to help plan larger projects.

Basic Steps to Follow

Materials:

- grid form on page 159
- 12" x 18" (30 x 46 cm) colored construction paper
- writing paper
- crayons or felt tip pens
- glue

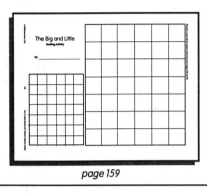

page 159

Directions:

Scaled Pictures

1. Create a design on the small grid. Color it in.

2. Create the same design on the larger grid. Be careful to scale the larger design accurately by counting the boxes on the grid.

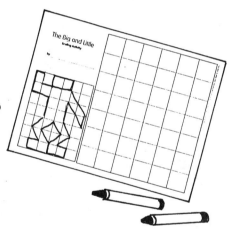

The Story

1. Develop a story about these diagrams.
How did the image grow larger? How did it shrink?
2. Copy the story in final form.

The Book

1. Each student folds the large sheet of construction paper in half. They glue the scaled picture on the top half and the story on the bottom half.

2. The construction paper folders are glued back-to-back.

3. Wrap a sheet of construction paper around the outside as a cover. Glue in place.

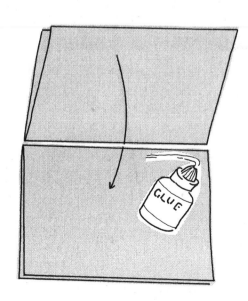

Tessellation Tricks

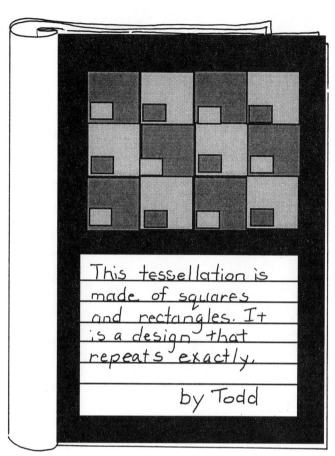

This tessellation is made of squares and rectangles. It is a design that repeats exactly.

by Todd

Project:

Creating tessellations is an interesting experience in patterning. The designs can be intricate or simple. These students' designs and stories are combined to create a class book that is everyone's favorite.

Topics:

1. Write a definition of - tessellation.

2. Describe the design you've created and explain why it qualifies as a tesselation.

What is it?

Tessellations are shapes that fit together without any spaces between them. The repetition of these shapes creates interesting visual effects.

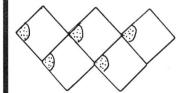

This is a tessellation.

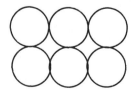

This is not a tessellation.

How to Make Books with Children-Science & Math

Basic Steps to Follow

Materials:

- 9" x 12" (23 x 30 cm) black construction paper
- writing paper
- 2" (5 cm) squares of red and yellow construction paper
- paste
- scissors
- pencil
- 9" x 12" (23 x 30 cm) yellow tagboard for a front and back cover
- hole punch
- 3 paper fasteners

Directions:

The Tessellation

1. Use the colored paper squares to develop a tessellation design. Cut and paste to create a pattern that repeats exactly. There can be no variation in shape. There may be variation in color. The designs may be simple or complex.

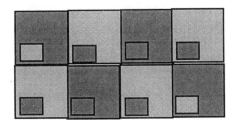

2. Paste the design to the top of the black construction paper.

The Story

1. Write a rough draft of the story, read it to a student editor and look for grammar and spelling errors. Copy the story in final form.

2. Paste it below the tessellation design.

The Book

1. Collect student designs and stories.
2. Create a hinged binding with the tagboard. (See page 3.) Punch holes and insert paper fasteners.

Dictionary of Math Terms

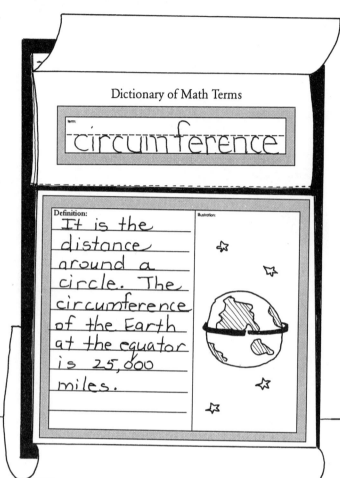

Dictionary of Math Terms

term: circumference

Definition:

It is the distance around a circle. The circumference of the Earth at the equator is 25,000 miles.

Illustration:

Project:

Topics:

Measurement Terms:	Geometric Terms:	Mathematical Terms:
volume	square	addition
area	circle	subtraction
perimeter	triangle	multiplication
diameter	oval	division
square feet	hexagon	estimation
circumference	rectangle	zero
inch	pentagon	place value
yard	quadrilateral	fractions
metric	angle	digit
Fahrenheit	sphere	regrouping
Celsius	cube	divisor
ounces	cylinder	dividend
gram	cone	equivalent

Basic Steps to Follow

Materials:

- the writing form on page 160
- 9" x 12" (23 x 30 cm) tagboard
- pencil
- felt tip pens
- scissors
- stapler

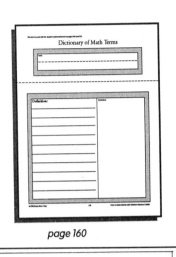

page 160

Directions:

Beginning
Brainstorm the vocabulary. Let each student pick a term and write a definition. Share the definitions and decide if they are clear and concise.

Inside Pages
Give each student a writing form. Have them complete the form for the mathematical term they have developed a definition. Let them add an illustration.

The Cover
1. Collect papers. Put them in **alphabetical** order.
Put a sheet of paper on top to be the cover sheet.

2. Staple the papers to the tagboard along the top edge.

3. Now cut loose the definition section of each paper on the dotted line.

4. Mix-up the loose pages so that they are out of order. Staple them to the tagboard along the bottom edge.

5. Share the book with other students. Can they guess which definition belongs to each term?

Compare and Contrast

Geometric Shapes

A Pop-Up Book

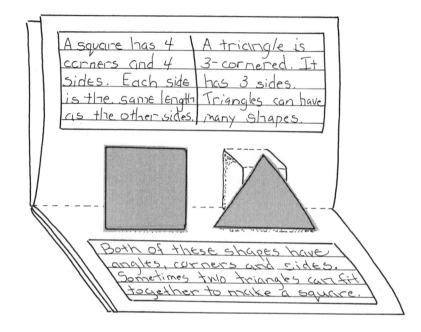

A square has 4 corners and 4 sides. Each side is the same length as the other sides.

A triangle is 3-cornered. It has 3 sides. Triangles can have many shapes.

Both of these shapes have angles, corners and sides. Sometimes two triangles can fit together to make a square.

Project:

This project gives students the opportunity to closely examine geometric shapes and their relationship to each other. Students describe two different shapes. Based on those descriptions, they are to compare similarities and differences of the shapes.

Topics:

Describe a shape.

square	pentagon
circle	quadrilateral
triangle	sphere
oval	cube
hexagon	cylinder
rectangle	cone

Compare two shapes.

Where are these shapes seen in nature?

         How to Make Books with Children-Science & Math

Basic Steps to Follow

Materials:

- 9" x 12" (23 x 30 cm) construction paper
- 3" x 4 1/2" (7 x 10 cm) pieces of various colors of construction paper
- 4" x 8" (9 x 21 cm) writing paper
- scissors
- glue
- one sheet of 9" x 12" (23 x 30 cm) construction paper for a cover

Directions:

The Pop-Up

1. Fold the white construction paper in half.

2. Cut two 1/2" (1.25 cm) tabs.

3. Fold the tabs back.

4. Push the tabs through to the reverse side.

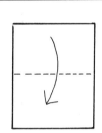

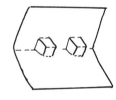
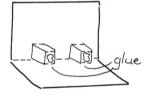

The Pop-Out Shapes

1. Students pick two shapes to compare and contrast.
They cut the shapes from the colorful construction paper.

2. The shapes are glued to the front of the tabs.
Place the glue on the tab and lay the shape on it.

The Writing

1. The student writes a description of each shape.
These descriptions are written on the writing paper strips.
Paste this strip to the background area of the pop-up.

2. Then the student compares the two shapes.
This writing paper is glued to the area below the pop-ups.

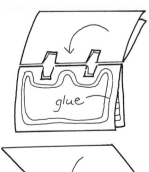

The Binding

Glue student pages back-to-back. Wrap a piece
of construction paper around the pop-up pages.

107   How to Make Books with Children-Science & Math

Magnets

Prehistoric Animals

your name:

paste picture here

dinosaur name:

family name:

time lived:

description:

_____

_____

_____

_____

_____

food preference:

_____

_____

_____

_____

habitat:

_____

_____

_____

_____

This form is used with the student-authored book on pages 10 and 11.

Archaeopteryx	Plesiosaurus	Compsognathus
Dimetrodon	Saber-Toothed Tiger	Giant Sloth
Eeohippus	Woolly Mammoth	Tyrannosaurus
Pteranodon	Stegosaurus	Apatosaurus

110

How to Make Books with Children-Science & Math

This form is used with the student-authored book on pages 10 and 11.

Ankylosaurus	Protoceratops	Iguanodon

Triceratops	Stegoceras	Rhamphorhynchus

Geosaurus	Zalambdalestes	Saurolophus

Psittacosaurus	Cariama	Diatryma

How to Make Books with Children-Science & Math

This form is used with the student-authored book on pages 12 and 13.

Pull-Tab
Pattern

This form is used with the
student-authored book on
pages 12 and 13.

pull down

pull down

Globe Pattern

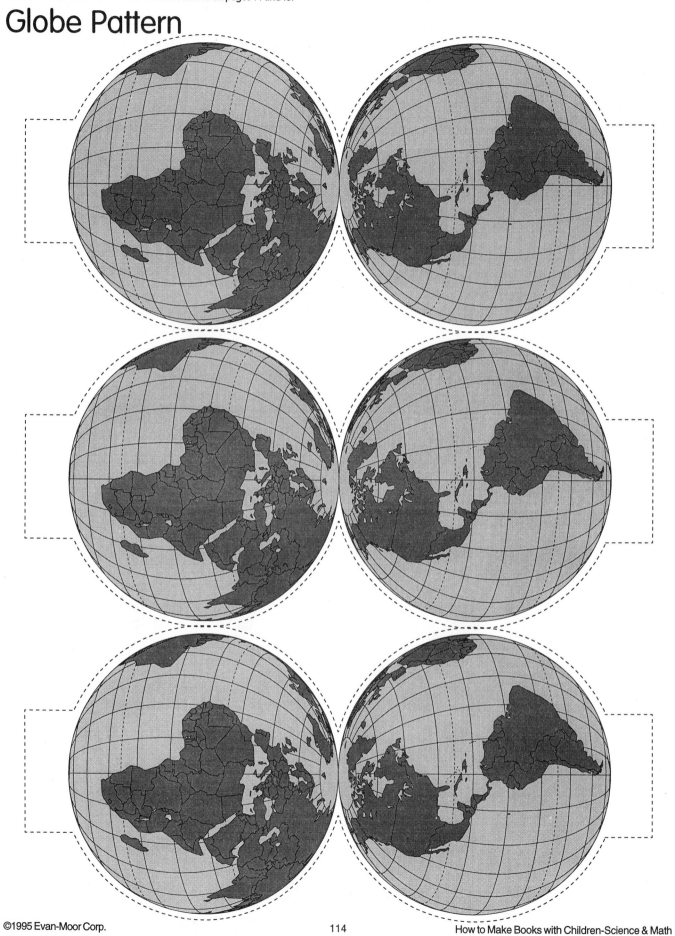

Light Bulb Pattern

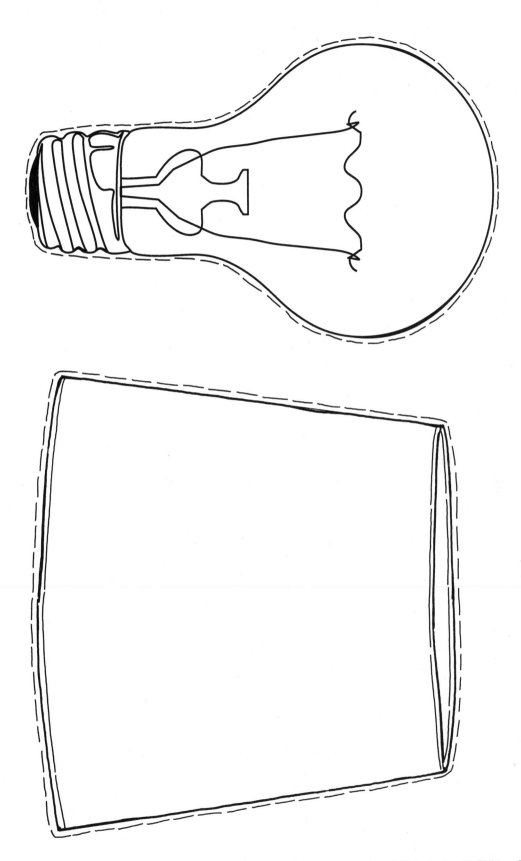

       How to Make Books with Children-Science & Math

This form is used with the student-authored book on pages 20 and 21.

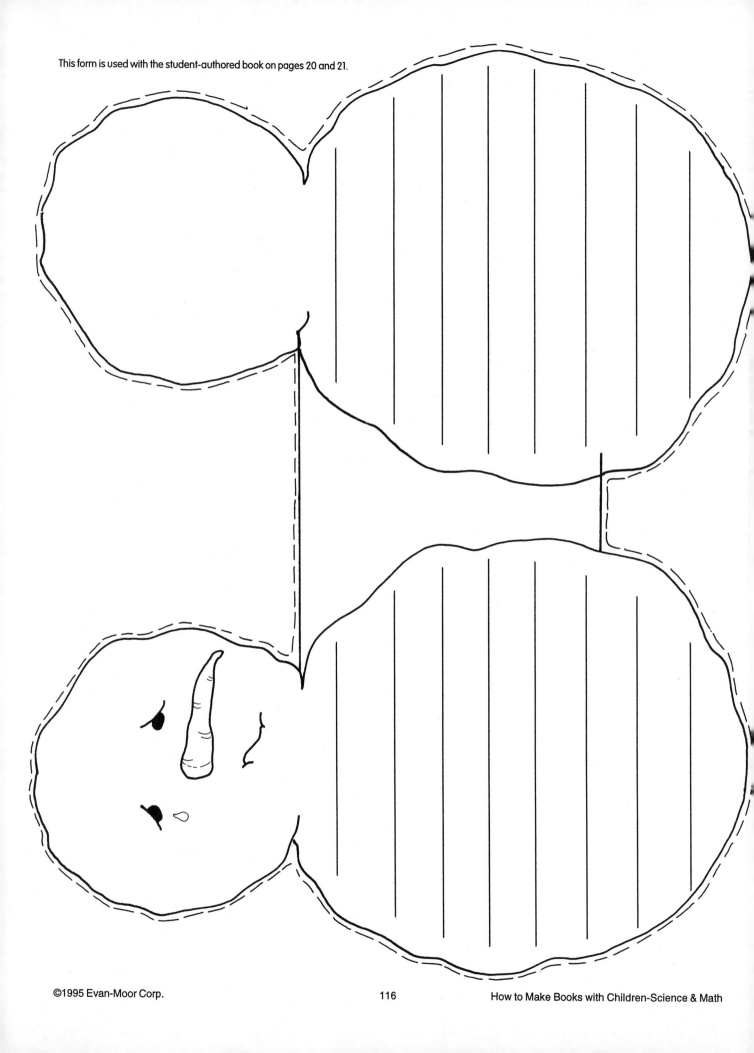

This form is used with the student-authored book on pages 22 and 23.

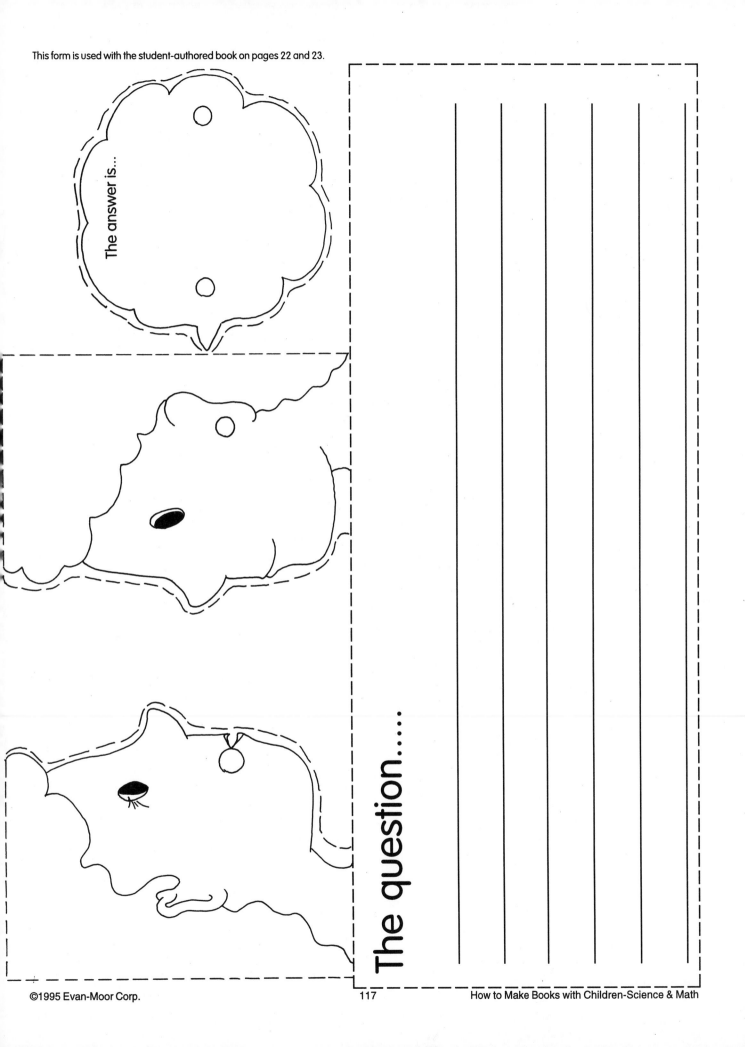

The answer is...

The question.....

How to Make Books with Children-Science & Math

Question:

_____

_____

_____

_____

1

_____

_____

_____

_____

2

_____

_____

_____

_____

3

_____

_____

_____

_____

4

_____

_____

_____

_____

Illustration

This form is used with the student-authored book on pages 32 and 33.

Before date

First Look date

Second Look date

Third Look date

What I know about mold:

Pop-Up
Pattern

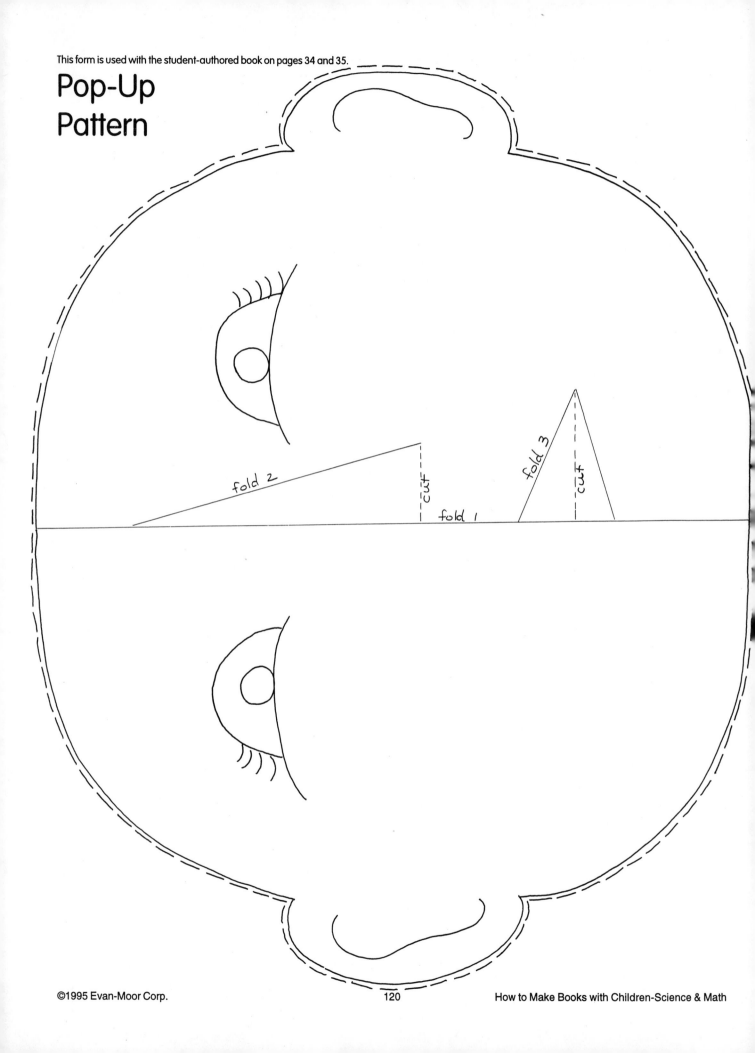

fold 2

cut

fold 1

fold 3

cut

name

1 taste

2 smell

3 hearing

4 sight

5 touch

MY FIVE SENSES

This form is used with the student-authored book on pages 36 and 37.

Scientific Opposites

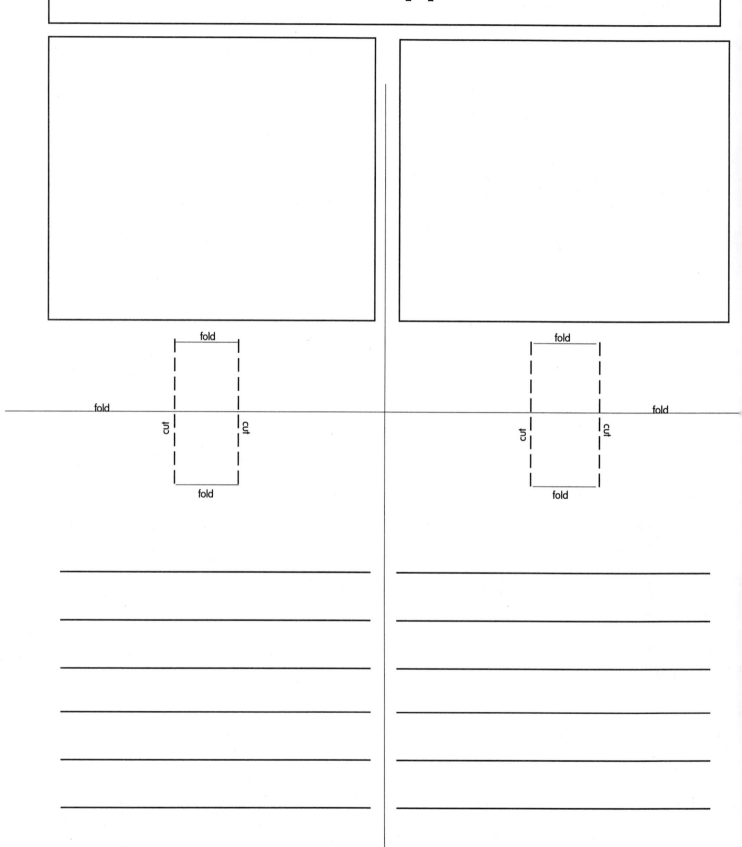

sink	float
sound	silence
dark	light
wet	dry

This form is used with the student-authored book on pages 42 and 43.

124

plant name:

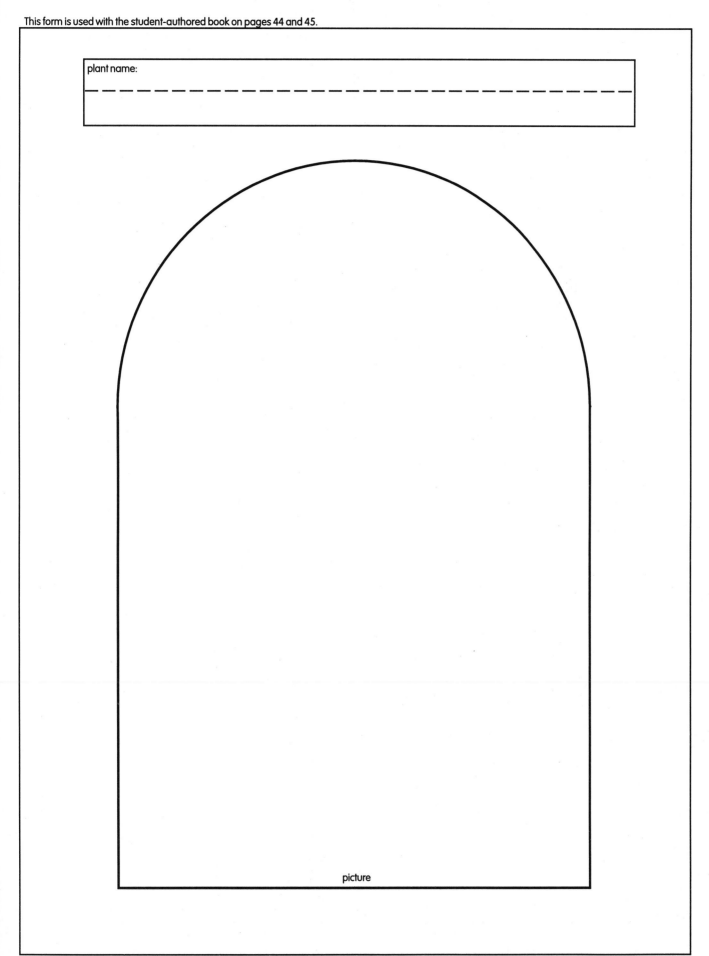

picture

This form is used with the student-authored book on pages 44 and 45.

Common Name:	Scientific Name:

Description:

_____

_____

_____

_____

_____

_____

Where and when to plant:

_____

_____

_____

How to plant:

_____

_____

_____

Check the type:

☐ annual
☐ perennial

☐ shade
☐ sun
☐ partial sun

☐ bulb
☐ seed
☐ vine
☐ bare root

Food and care:

_____

_____

_____

_____

Name:

A Report on Camouflage

What it is and what it does:

_____

_____

_____

_____

_____

_____

_____

_____

List the different types of camouflage that nature provides:

_____

_____

_____

_____

_____

_____

Name animals that use camouflage as a protective device:

_____

_____

_____

Does man utilize the protective aspects of camouflage?

_____

_____

_____

The Law of Gravity

What is it?

_____

_____

_____

_____

How does it operate?

_____

_____

_____

_____

_____

Where does it operate?

_____

_____

Who discovered it?

_____

_____

_____

by _____

This form is used with the student-authored book on pages 48 and 49.

with gravity

without gravity

Who am I?

_____

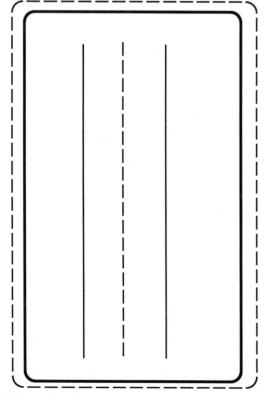

Here is the picture:

Here is the answer:

_____

What It Does

_____

_____

_____

_____

_____

_____

 How to Make Books with Children-Science & Math

How It Does It

_____

_____

_____

_____

_____

_____

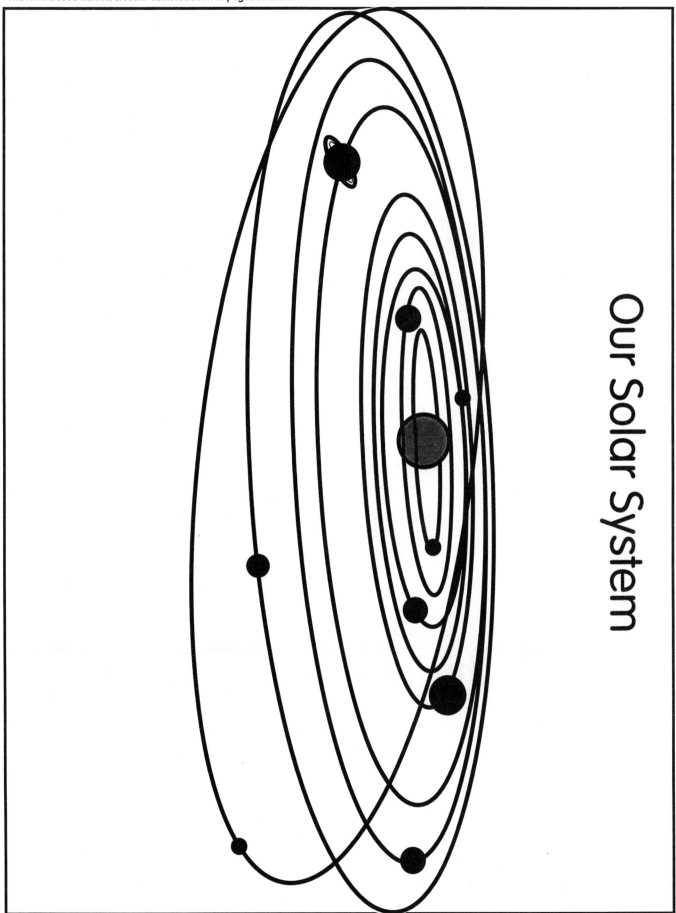

Our Solar System

This form is used with the student-authored book on pages 60 and 61.

Before

After

Why did this happen?

How did that happen?

The answer is...

1. _____

2. _____

3. _____

This form is used with the student-authored book on pages 62 and 63.

Pull-Tab Pattern

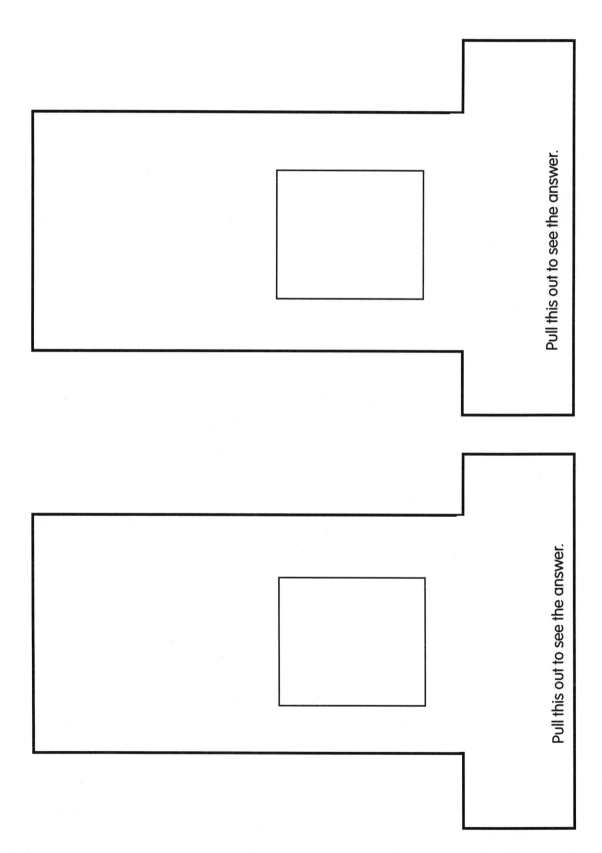

How We Got the Job Done

Job I need to do:

_____

_____

_____

Problem:

_____

_____

_____

_____

- -

Solution: What simple machines would help me do the job?

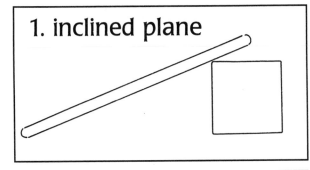
1. inclined plane

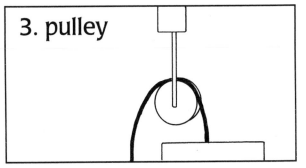
3. pulley

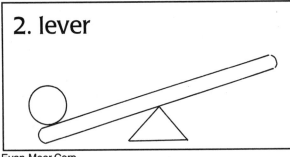
2. lever

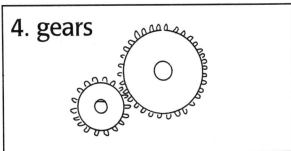
4. gears

What it is

What it does
How it does it

Where it is

This form is used with the student-authored book on pages 70 and 71.

name: _____

Group:

Animals in this group:

Characteristics:

autumn   autumn   autumn

summer

winter

paste

summer

winter

summer

winter

summer

winter

spring   spring   spring

autumn
in the northern hemisphere

spring
in the northern hemisphere

summer
in the northern hemisphere

winter
in the northern hemisphere

autumn
in the northern hemisphere

spring
in the northern hemisphere

summer
in the northern hemisphere

winter
in the northern hemisphere

autumn
in the northern hemisphere

spring
in the northern hemisphere

summer
in the northern hemisphere

winter
in the northern hemisphere

autumn
in the northern hemisphere

spring
in the northern hemisphere

summer
in the northern hemisphere

winter
in the northern hemisphere

Volcano Patterns

This form is used with the student-authored book on pages 74 and 75.

How:

_____

_____

_____

_____

_____

_____

_____

Where:

_____

_____

_____

_____

_____

_____

How to Make Books with Children-Science & Math

This form is used with the student-authored book on pages 74 and 75.

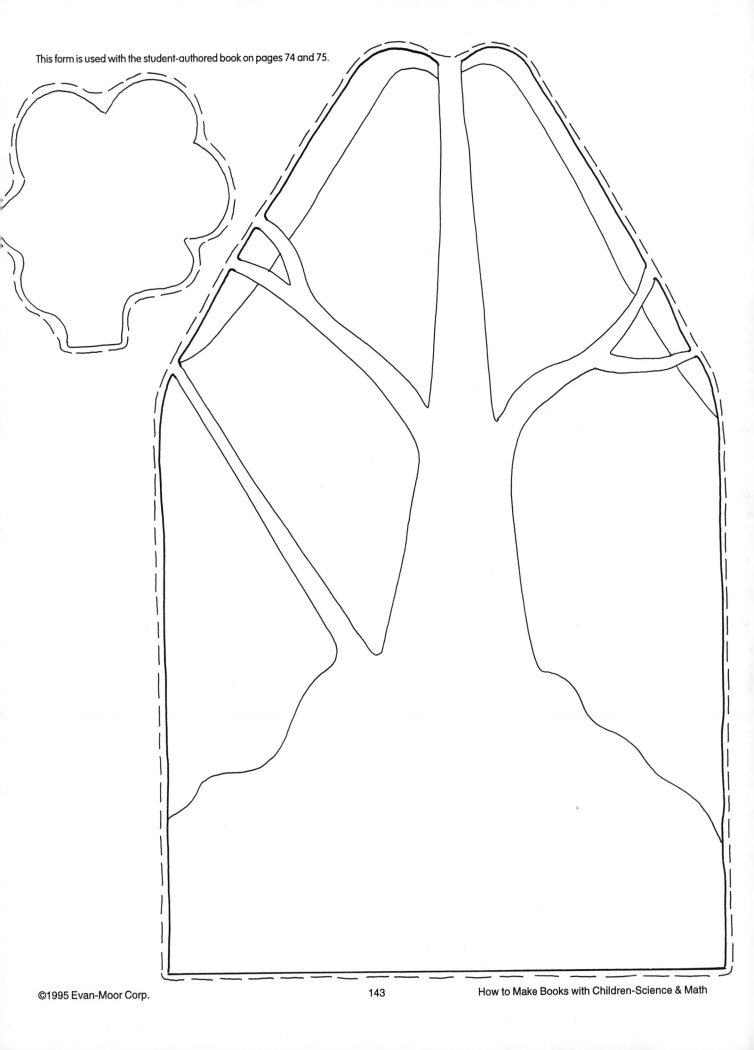

How to Make Books with Children-Science & Math

This form is used with the student-authored book on pages 80 and 81.

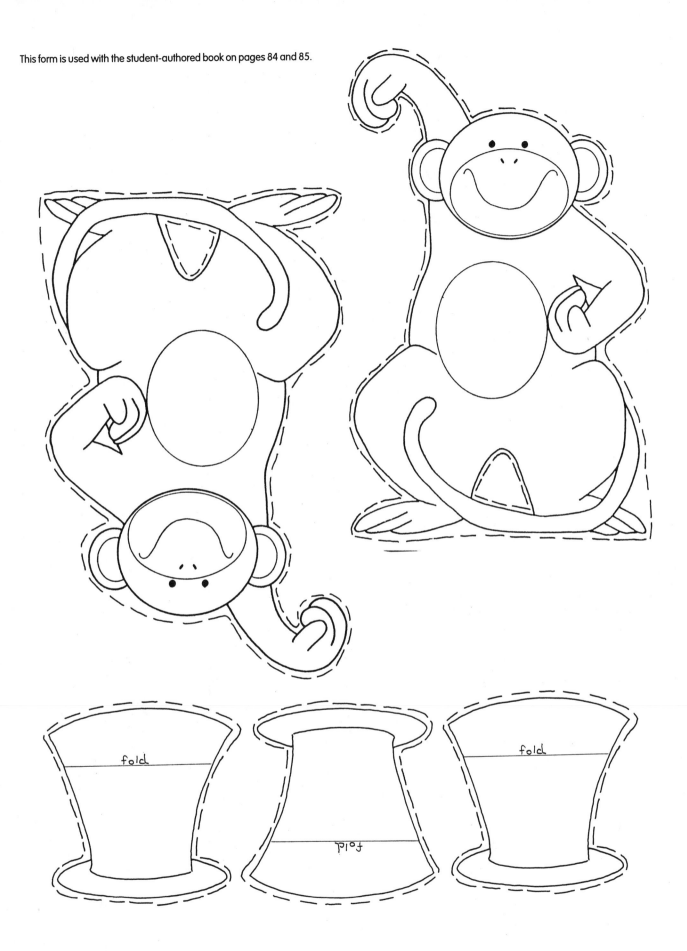

fold

plot

fold

paste

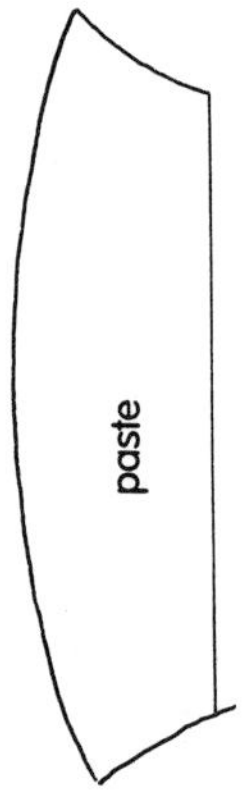

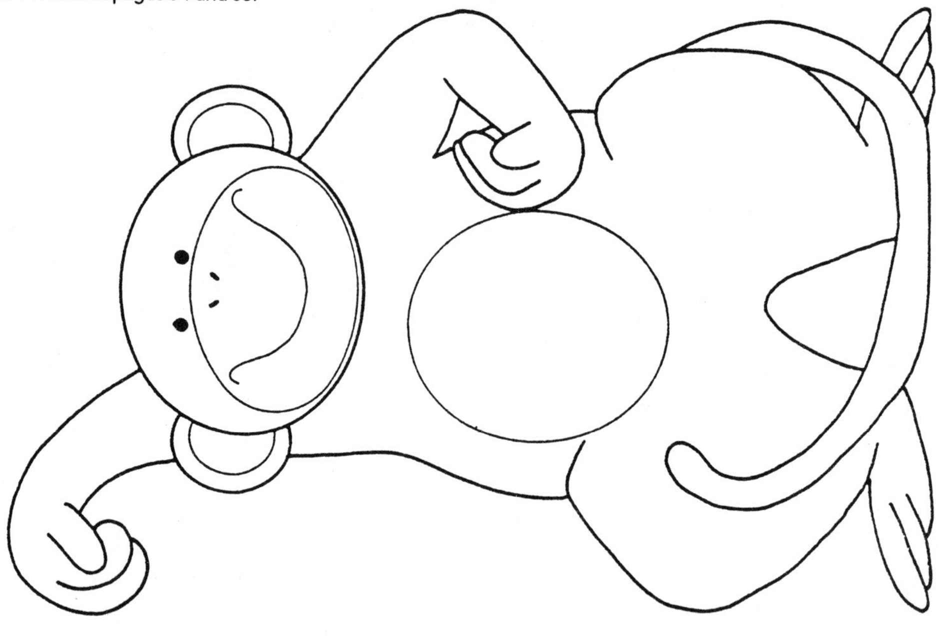

Can you guess? What is under the monkey's hat?

Name

This form is used with the student-authored book on pages 88 and 89.

How Many Were Left?

by _____

How to Make Books with Children-Science & Math

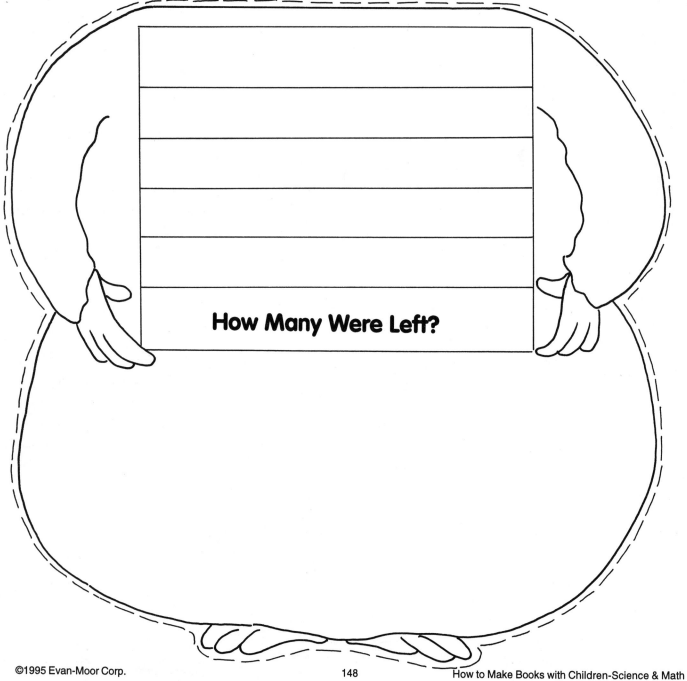

How Many Were Left?

This form is used with the student-authored book on pages 90 and 91.

by

Answer Box

Answer Box

Centimeter Worm

1
2
3
4
5
6
7
8
9
10
11
12
13
14
15
16
17
18
19
20
21
22

Inch Worm

1
2
3
4
5
6
7
8

How to Make Books with Children-Science & Math

measure measure measure measure measure

measure

measure

measure

measure

measure

measure

measure

measure

measure

measure

measure measure measure measure measure

How to Make Books with Children-Science & Math

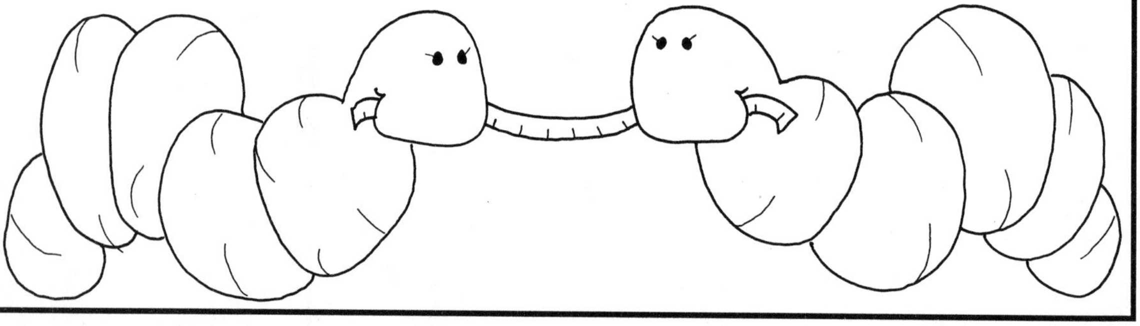

Cut It Up Patterns

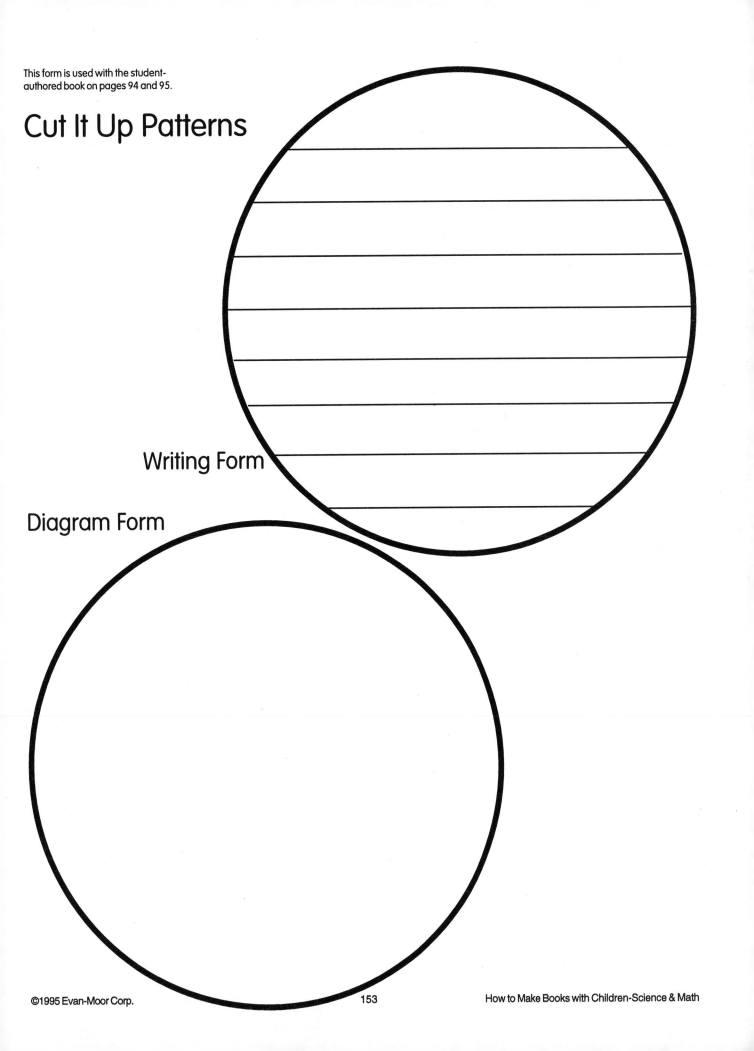

Writing Form

Diagram Form

This form is used with the student-authored book on pages 96 and 97.

My Recipe

Name:

Name of Recipe:

Ingredients:

Steps to follow:

This form is used with the student-authored book on pages 96 and 97.

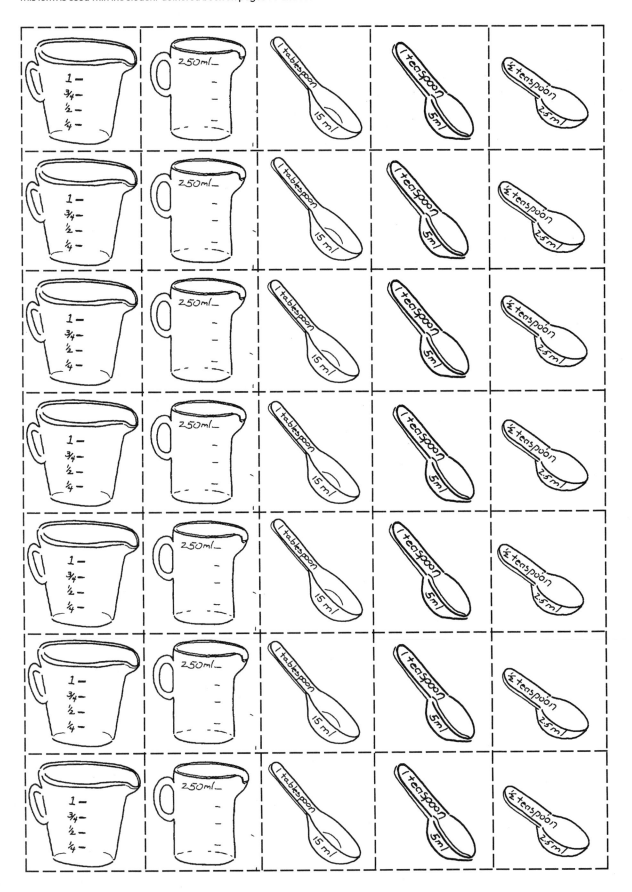

How to Make Books with Children-Science & Math

This form is used with the student-authored book on pages 98 and 99.

How to Make Books with Children-Science & Math

This form is used with the student-authored book on pages 98 and 99.

How to Make Books with Children-Science & Math

This form is used with the student-authored book on pages 98 and 99.

Build a 1,000

Build a 1,000

Build a 1,000

The Big and Little
Scaling Activity

by _____

Dictionary of Math Terms

term:

- -

- -

Definition:

illustration: